A Dedicant's Guide to 1st Degree Priesthood

The First Step to Clergy in the Craft of the Wise

A Dedicant's Guide to 1st Degree Priesthood

The First Step to Clergy in the Craft of the Wise

M.L. Rosenblad

MOON
BOOKS

Winchester, UK
Washington, USA

First published by Moon Books, 2014
Moon Books is an imprint of John Hunt Publishing Ltd., Laurel House, Station Approach,
Alresford, Hants, SO24 9JH, UK
office1@jhpbooks.net
www.johnhuntpublishing.com
www.moon-books.net

For distributor details and how to order please visit the 'Ordering' section on our website.

Text copyright: M.L. Rosenblad 2013

ISBN: 978 1 78279 364 9

A CIP catalogue record for this book is available from the British Library.

Design: Lee Nash

Printed in the USA by Edwards Brothers Malloy

We operate a distinctive and ethical publishing philosophy in all areas of our business, from our global network of authors to production and worldwide distribution.

CONTENTS

To my loving wife Chris,
without her support and understanding;
this project would have never been started.

Introduction

In this book, you will begin your walk on the Path to Pagan Priesthood. It is not a short or easy journey. There is much to be learned. Some of what you read, you may already have an understanding of, but it is provided here to help you understand its value and add to your knowledge as you grow.

Much of what you will learn on this road comes from many different Paths. This is done to allow you, as a member of the Clergy, to be better rounded and to provide you with a better understanding of the many belief systems around you.

It is not the intention of this course to teach a single-minded system, but rather to enlighten the student to the fact that all Paths have merit.

Take what you learn here to heart. Know that this road is one that leads to a great responsibility. The general public holds you, as a member of the Clergy, to a much higher standard. Your knowledge and the presentation of yourself are reflections on your chosen Path.

Namaste

Phase One

Simple Beginnings

Just as a candle cannot burn without fire, men cannot live without a spiritual life.
Buddha

The decision to travel the Path to Clergy is not one to be taken lightly. It is a Path of challenges, self-examination and constant learning. As a member of the Clergy, you will be a leader, a teacher, a confidant and a guide. These roles require a deep-seated commitment and a strong desire for self-growth.

The lessons contained in this book are designed to familiarize you with the basic ideas and tenets of Wiccan philosophy. You will be provided the information needed to become a 1st Degree Priest/Priestess in our Alliance. Upon completion of your studies there will be a written test based on the material you have learned, followed by an oral interview with the Alliance Directorship. Successful completion of all phases is required to be granted initiation into the 1st Degree Clergy.

Core Subjects

As a 1st Degree Priest/Priestess, you are required to have a basic knowledge of certain ideals, tenets and documents that are a large part of the Tradition's philosophy. As a member of the Priesthood, you may be called upon to help others learn and grow. The ability to speak clearly on these subjects is quite important and, as such, must be committed to your heart and mind. These subjects are as follows:

- The Wiccan Rede
- Grounding and centering
- **Altar Tools and their meaning**
- **Associated Altar** tools
- **The Altar**
- Deity

The Wiccan Rede

Full Version

Bide within the Law you must, in perfect Love and perfect Trust. Live you must and let to live, fairly take and fairly give. For tread the Circle thrice about to keep unwelcome spirits out. To bind the spell well every time, let the spell be said in rhyme. Light of eye and soft of touch, speak you little, listen much. Honor the Old Ones in deed and name, let love and light be our guides again. Deosil go by the waxing moon, chanting out the joyful tune. Widdershins go when the moon doth wane, and the werewolf howls by the dread wolfsbane. When the Lady's moon is new, kiss the hand to Her times two. When the moon rides at Her peak, then your heart's desire seek. Heed the North wind's mighty gale, lock the door and trim the sail. When the wind blows from the East, expect the new and set the feast. When the wind comes from the South, love will kiss you on the mouth. When the wind whispers from the West, all hearts will find peace and rest. Nine woods in the Cauldron go, burn them fast and burn them slow. Birch in the fire goes to represent what the Lady knows. Oak in the forest towers with might, in the fire it brings the God's insight. Rowan is a tree of power causing life and magick to flower. Willows at the waterside stand ready to help us to the Summerland. Hawthorn is burned to purify and to draw faerie to your eye. Hazel, the tree of wisdom and learning, adds its strength to the bright fire burning. White are the flowers of Apple tree that brings us fruits of fertility. Grapes grow upon the vine giving us both joy and wine. Fir does mark the evergreen to represent immortality seen. Elder is the Lady's tree, burn it not or cursed you'll be. Four times the Major Sabbats mark in the light and in the dark. As the old year starts to wane the new begins, it's now Samhain. When the time for Imbolc shows watch for flowers through the snows. When the wheel begins to turn soon the Beltane fires will burn. As the wheel turns to Lamas night power is brought to magick rite. Four times the Minor Sabbats fall, use the Sun to mark them all. When the wheel has turned to Yule light the log the Horned One rules. In the spring, when night equals day, time for Ostara to come our way. When the Sun has reached its height, time for Oak and Holly to fight. Harvesting comes to one and all when the Autumn Equinox does fall. Heed the flower, bush, and tree by the Lady blessed you'll be. Where the rippling waters go cast a stone, the truth you'll know. When you have and hold a need, harken not to others' greed. With a fool no season spend or be counted as his friend. Merry Meet and Merry Part, bright the cheeks and warm the heart. Mind the Three-fold Laws you should, three times bad and three times good. When misfortune is enow wear the star upon your brow. Be true in love this you must do unless your love is false to you. **These Eight words the Rede fulfill: 'An Ye Harm None, Do What Ye Will'.**

As you read and learn this, ask yourself; what is the meaning? In what part of my life as a member of the Priesthood will these words best serve the Tradition and myself? The version used by most followers of the Path is the one shown here. It was first published by Doreen Valiente after a speech that contained it. Many will argue that the Rede is much older, that there are many instances of this document's wording found in literature that pre-date her publishing of it. The Rede is a poem written to make the basic ideas of the Pagan philosophy more readily understood. It is based on ideals and tenets that are much older. You must remember that the Rede was written at a time when England had just repealed the old witchcraft laws and many were still concerned about this. As a poem instead of a set of rules, the Rede was looked at as more of a literary work by the mainstream population of the time.

The Rede teaches us that we are free to choose what we do in our life, but cautions us to think before acting. Each must ask themselves; can my actions or words have a harmful effect? This harm does not have to be immediate; it may present itself down the road of life. When we speak of harm, we are not limiting the word to another person; but to all things including ourselves. If, in the course of your contemplation, you feel your action or inaction can do harm then would it be prudent to do what you were planning or take a different course of action?

The rule of three speaks of what most know as karmic return. This statement does not mean you will get back three times what you have sent out (good or bad), but rather it implies that you will, over a period of time (perhaps lifetimes), receive the equivalent of what you have done until Deity determines you have learned your lesson or have been given the proper reward for your actions.

Throughout the Rede, the words speak of honor, honesty and compassion. These tenets should be held most high in all you do or say. It also tells us that we should always strive to learn and grow. No one person can ever know or understand everything, school is always in session.

As a Tradition, we strive to follow the principles set forth in the Rede, as members of the Priesthood; we must demonstrate the Rede in our day-to-day lives. It is our job to lead through example and, by simply following the Rede, we are well on our way to being good custodians of the Wiccan Faith.

Grounding and Centering

As is taught in the Introduction to Wicca, grounding and centering are vital tools for clearing our minds and bodies of negative energy and focusing our energies to any given task. It allows us to achieve a state of calm that will help us enter a higher state of consciousness. This higher consciousness gives us the key to using the energies found both within ourselves and in all things around us.

On the Path to Priesthood, we begin to learn to use these outer and inner energies in a much more physical way. It becomes much less of a mental exercise to aid us in our endeavors and becomes a tool allowing us to progress along a magickal path as well as giving us the ability to teach in a more positive manner.

This process also allows us to be much more effective in divination and is absolutely necessary for being used as an oracle. A lack of focus or a distracted mind will cause an inaccurate divination, which could actually end up doing harm. Keep this in the forefront of your mind.

There are numerous ways to accomplish grounding and centering, as is taught in the Introduction to Wicca. Simply choose what works best for you and proceed. Visualize an image of energy growing in your mind until it manifests itself on the physical plane (many use a lit candle to direct their focus in this process). See it flowing into and through you. This will allow you to feel and see the cleansing energies flow through you, drawing off all negativity down through your body and entering the ground beneath you, allowing the energies of the Earth to charge them for later use.

As you are in the process of the visualization to aid you in Grounding, allow the energy you have called upon to help remove the mundane from your mind. In doing this, your mind will be able to better focus on the tasks ahead and aid you in being successful in your endeavors. At the end of this Phase of learning, you will find practice techniques to aid you in the process of Grounding and Centering. Ultimately you may develop a style, which will fit you more readily. This is the beginning of growth within the Path you have chosen to follow.

Grounding and centering are not just tools for ritual practice; they are tools you can use in your day-to-day life to aid you in anything you must do. The increase in focus you receive from these techniques will work positively for you in a multitude of ways.

Altar Tools and Their Meanings

There are many things that a Priest can use and place on their Altar, in this section; we will describe the essentials and their meanings. The tools you place on your Altar should be cleansed and charged prior to their first use and occasionally recharged to keep them clear of negative energy. (A cleansing Ritual can be found at the end of this phase).

Each tool you choose should be special to you as a Priest, a gift from someone, a found item that spoke out to you, etc. Using these kinds of tools will enhance the energies within your space and will aid in banishing negativity from the Circle. Any of the tools mentioned in this section will contain more of your personal energy if they are made by your own hand. If you have the talent to do this, it is recommended that you do. That does not mean that commercially obtained tools will not work, they will do just fine.

Athame

The Athame is the primary tool of the Witch. It symbolizes the God and is therefore considered masculine in nature. It can be used to call the Circle, allows the Witch to create a doorway to safely leave the Circle without first closing it. It can be used to close the Circle and is used in many spells and incantations. It is a blade or knife, but it may never be used to cut anything and should be protected at all costs. It is not necessary for this blade to have a sharp edge, in fact; a blunt edge may even be preferable. Your Athame may be commercially produced or made by the user. Obviously, making it yourself will imbue it with your own essence. This will allow the blade to be in tune with you. This tool can be made of wood, stone, metal or any combination of these materials. Basically, this item is essentially a medium to long-bladed knife. Usually, the hilt (handle) is black. This is significant, because it demonstrates a blending of all of the primary colors. That allows the blade to absorb and store energies for later use. Whether you choose to buy it commercially or make it yourself, the blade must be charged and blessed. This blade has a very deep symbolic nature and should be stored in a manner that does not allow it to make contact with any of your other Altar tools.

Boline

The Boline is simply a knife that may be used for cutting objects that will be used in rituals, spells, etc. Its edge should be kept quite sharp so as to not tear that which is to be cut (the sharpening stone for this tool should be used for no other purpose than sharpening the Boline). This tool may never be used to cut anything living; it must never be used to draw blood or touch blood in any way and must be purified and charged just as the Athame.

It must never be used outside of its designated purpose, to do so would damage the purification and charging. The blade's primary use is to cut plants or other things to be used in Magickal practice and Rituals (herbs, plants, etc.).

Your Boline can be any commercially available small knife with a fixed blade. It may be any type of knife you choose, be it double-edged, single-edged, curved or straight; but it should never have a serrated edge. The color of the hilt should not be black as in the Athame. It need not be fancy as it is merely a cutting tool and requires nothing special other than being charged and purified.

Chalice

The Chalice is symbolic of the Goddess and is considered a feminine form. It embodies nurturing and fertility. It may be used for offering a gift to Goddess for her presence within your Circle as well as a part of many rituals.

This tool may be made of glass, metal or any other material capable of containing liquids. As with anything, it must be charged and blessed, and never used for any purpose outside Ritual.

In storage, regardless of the material it is made from, it should be wrapped and not made to make actual contact with any of the other tools. The Chalice, like the Athame, is of a special nature and should be handled with special care and the respect due their symbolic nature.

Cauldron/Thurible

This will usually cause a person to imagine a large black metal pot boiling away on the fire, but that is not so in this case. This item would be a small fireproof container used for the burning of incense. Incense represents the Element of Air and should always be present during Ritual. The container you choose should be appropriate to the type of incense you are using (cone, powder, etc.), so as not to cause a fire on the Altar. You should not consider the embers of the incense as representing the Element of Fire, it is merely the transmission device for the smoke of the incense, which represents the Element Air.

Two Elemental Bowls

In these you place salt in one, representing the Element Earth and in the other water, obviously representing the Element Water. You need not put much in either bowl, as waste is offensive to Goddess. In many Rituals (most in fact), the water is blended with the salt and asperged around the Circle to cleanse the area of any negativity that has entered the sacred space with the attendees.

Candles

Two candles (in appropriate holders) should always be present on the Altar. They serve a dual purpose. They can represent the

Element Fire and are also symbolic of the Goddess and God. These candles are a representation of the presence of Deity at your Ritual. If at all possible, once lit, the candles should be allowed to burn themselves out naturally. In the event this is not practical, you should use a candle snuffer. Blowing out a Ritual candle has long been considered disrespectful to both the Goddess and God.

You may add other items of meaning to your Altar, but these are the tools that should never be left out. They are extremely important to raising and containing the energies of your Circle and aiding in successful Ritual.

Associated Altar Tools

There are a number of other Altar tools that you may add. The ones listed here are tools that, while important and useful, are not absolutely necessary for a successful Ritual.

Once again, there are numerous other items you may add to your Altar. Those would be a matter of personal preference but should carry with them a special meaning to you.

Besom

The Besom is essentially an old-world crafted broom. This tool is used in clearing away the debris of negative energy. Since it is a broom, you would appropriately think it is to be used in a sweeping manner just as any other broom. This is true... to a point. The bristles of the Besom should never touch the floor during an energy clearing; you should sweep the air space just above the floor/ground in the space that you are going to use (ordinarily, a chant will accompany this Ritual sweeping). This is very important because contact with the ground can cause the Besom to absorb the negative energies in the area, which would require the tool to be recharged and purified.

Many commercially made Besoms are available and, if properly cleansed and purified before being put to use, are perfectly fine. Once again, as with any tool you may use, if you have the ability to make it yourself; it will contain the power of your essence and only become a stronger tool in your hands.

Wand

This tool is one of the most misunderstood of all Magickal tools. It is thought by a great many people to contain Magickal powers; in fact it, by itself, does not. The Wand is an instrument used for directing energy that has been brought into focus towards an intended goal or object. It essentially acts as a metaphysical pointing laser. There are a great many Wands available, quite a few made for specific purposes, from very select materials. These can be quite ornate and somewhat expensive. A good, general purpose Wand can be something found in nature and finished by you. As always, one that is made by your own hand will carry with it more of your own essence and power.

Choosing a wood for its associated Magickal ability is a good plan and wood properties will be covered a bit later. The one thing that you are advised in this area now is not to use wood from the Yew tree. That particular wood is associated with death and dark forces.

Some will place a crystal or stone on the end of their wand (choose well, based on the attributes of the stone or crystal), others will even choose to use a crystal rod and adorn it with items of Magickal value. Most metals are not acceptable (some base metals have specific Magickal properties) for use in wands. There are certain exceptions and those will be discussed later in your training. Whatever you decide, remember to consider what you use or purchase; in the right hands, this can be a very powerful instrument.

Altar Sword

Swords are a symbol of the God, just as an Athame and are often used to cast the Circle. It carries the same requirements as an Athame, but requires considerably more space for storage and can be quite heavy.

If you choose to keep a sword in your altar supplies, treat it as you would your athame and remember, it does not replace the Athame but rather is used in complement to it. You should also know that there are areas whereby transporting a Sword can lead to legal issues, so if you are traveling check locals laws. It is a tool used in Religious practice, but it can also slow down your travels until the validity of your Clergy status is determined.

Singing Bowl

Singing bowls have long been used in Buddhist culture as a means of focusing and achieving alignment with the higher self, using the seventh method for attaining enlightenment, sound. The vibrations emanating from a singing bowl during use can produce a state of calm and healing that allows easy transition to the higher self. The vibration (sound) is caused by moving the mallet around the outside of the bowl or a very light tap of the mallet to the outside of the bowl. By varying the speed and pressure of the mallet, you can alter the resonance of the sound and find the vibration that has the best effect and allows for transition.

The singing bowl has been in use since Buddhism was introduced in Tibet around the 8th century C.E. when the third incarnation of Buddha visited the region from India.

Pentagram

Many Wiccans/Pagans use the pentagram as a symbol of faith similar to the Christian Cross. It is not, however, a universal symbol for Paganism. Its religious symbolism is commonly explained by reference to the neo-Pythagorean understanding that the five vertices of the pentagram represent the four elements (Earth, Air, Water and Fire) with the addition of Spirit as the uppermost point. As a representation of the elements, the pentagram is involved in the Wiccan practice of summoning the elemental spirits of the four directions at the beginning of a ritual.

The Altar

The altar is the focal point of any ritual. It is the energy center and offering point. Some practitioners maintain a personal Altar in their homes, if space allows, as a display of respect to Deity.

Your Altar may be as simple or as elaborate as you choose. There are as many variations as there are practitioners.

Some Traditions teach that the altar should be set up in a manner dividing the left side from the right side to show the feminine and masculine aspects of Deity separately. If this is the method you choose, it is important to remember that the left side of your Altar represents Goddess (feminine) while the right side represents the God (masculine).

Positioning of your Altar is also very important. Many choose to always face the Altar to the North. However, there are proponents who say it is important to face the Altar in the direction of the desired quality to be called upon during Ritual, be that aspect knowledge or strength, etc. Other techniques of placing your Altar use Geomancy, Feng Shui and other practices to achieve placement in alignment with the appropriate energies.

Most will place an altar cloth over the top of their altar. If you do, choose an Altar cloth that demonstrates meaning to you. This will only increase the energy of your Altar by drawing from your energy and intent.

The material your Altar is made from can directly affect the power and energy of the Altar itself. A metal Altar top can diffuse the energy that you impart to your tools and therefore is not a desirable material for use. Wood or stone are the preferred materials for your Altar top as they maintain the contact to Earth and the energies contained therein. The type of wood or stone you would use for this purpose can vary greatly, but should be chosen based on the properties of the material. These things will be covered later in your 1st Degree training.

Deity

When we speak of Deity, we are speaking of something that encompasses all things. All things tangible and intangible, both past and present. We are speaking of Goddess in her purest form. Deity appears to us in many forms. The many Gods and Goddesses of myth and folklore manifest as a whisper inside of you. She is a guide and a confidante. In our personal relationship with Deity, she comes to us in a form that we can relate to. Every individual will see Deity in his or her own personal way. Because of this many assume there are a multitude of Gods and Goddesses when in fact we are each seeing a slightly different view of the same Deity.

We live many lifetimes, through reincarnation. Sometimes we react very strongly to a specific view of Deity because we have interacted with Deity through that face in one or more past lifetimes.

There are two levels to the Wiccan understanding of Deity. The first is personal, the second universal. On the personal level we see the Divine as an entity that we interact with through words and actions and with whom we maintain a personal relationship. At this level we give Deity many names and faces, and interact with Deity through these. Most Wiccans will use a variety of names and faces for Deity in this personal sense, and will have one particular form, which they perceive as their personal Deity. They will interact with this vision of Deity, or sometimes a variety of Deities, looking to that aspect of the Divine for guidance, inspiration, and practical help in both daily life and our spiritual path.

The second way in which Wiccans look at Deity is universal. We acknowledge that the true nature of Deity cannot truly be named, and is perhaps beyond all our understanding. As our personal images of Deity are the varied reflections, so Universal

Deity is the mirror. Wiccans believe that any one name or form for Deity can never possibly encompass all of the nature of Universal Deity, but can only serve to limit our understanding of it. We use our personal images of Deity symbolically to help us understand the nature of Universal Deity, using our personal view as a tool to define the qualities and actions of the Divine without ever imagining that a single view can possibly capture the whole nature of Deity.

Glossary of Pagan/Wiccan Terms

Athame: A witch's black handled ritual knife. It is never used to cut anything. It is used to direct energy and occasionally to inscribe runes and other symbols into candles. It is also used to dip into water to represent the union of the Goddess and the God in the great rite. The Magick knife.

Adept: Someone who through study and experience is highly proficient in something.

Akashic Records: Records kept on the Astral plane of each and every human life and all our past lives. It is believed you can access these records to look into your past lives and the future.

Amulet: A Magickally charged object for protection (different from a Talisman).

Astral Plane: The plane that interpenetrates and reflects our physical plane, but operates on a higher frequency. Magickal workings are done in the Astral plane to affect the physical plane. When casting a Circle you do so on the Astral Plane to protect you on both the Astral and Physical planes.

Astral Projection: Projecting your Astral body (soul/spirit) out from the physical body.

Balefire: A fire lit for a magickal purpose.

Bane: Bad. That which destroys life.

Besom: A witch's broom, usually round, over which a couple jump during a handfasting or used to 'sweep' away bad energy. It is never used to actually sweep the floor, it instead sweeps negativity away.

Boline: A knife (with handle colored other than black) used to cut herbs and other plants for ritual work; the Working knife.

Book of Shadows (B.O.S): The book that contains all the magickal information, spells, rites, herbal information, herbal recipes of a Witch. Sometimes called a Grimoire. This has been replaced by computer folders and disks in some cases.

Cairn: A pillar of rocks. Usually nine or eleven.

Call: Another term for invoking

Cauldron: Preferably a cast iron pot, but even a bowl can do. It represents the Goddess and is often filled with flowers and water. It is often used for scrying.

Censer: A heatproof container in which incense is burnt. It represents the Element Air.

Chakra: 'Wheel of light'. There are seven main Chakras in the body: crown, third eye, throat, heart, solar plexus, navel, base. They are energy centers of the body.

Clairaudience: Being able to hear messages.

Clairsentience: Being able to 'feel' or 'know' messages (also called the power of prophecy). Sometimes a clairsentient person can perceive smells, taste or touch.

Clairvoyant: Being able to see messages through inner sight.

Cleansing: Removing negativity, either on the astral plane (using white light etc.) or on the physical plane (using salt etc.)

Cone of Power: The energy that is raised in a Magick Circle. It is done by chanting/singing/drumming/walking etc. The energy is focused on a goal, then built up and sent out through the top of the circle into the astral plane to work its power.

Consecration: A process of cleansing an object and blessing it in the names of the Goddess and/or God for Magickal/religious use.

Corn dolly - A dolly made from corn husks (some books I have read say that American 'corn' is actually wheat). A symbol of the Goddess, especially at Beltane.

Coven: A group of three or more Witches, traditionally 13, who get together for Esbats and other rituals/meetings. Usually led by a female (High Priestess) and a male (High Priest). Members of a coven are referred to as Priests or Priestesses.

Covenstead: The meeting place of a coven (if not outdoors), or the High Priestess's house.

Deosil: Also called 'sunwise'. The direction the sun travels in the sky. In the Northern Hemisphere it is clockwise, in the Southern

Hemisphere it is counter-clockwise.

Divination: To see into the future using tools such as a cauldron, tarot cards, I Ching, Runes etc.

Divining: The use of divination (i.e. he was divining using his Tarot cards).

Elementals: The personification of the Elements. Earth = Gnomes, Fire = Salamanders (some books have said they are fire spirits some have said they are the lizards), Water = Undines (mermaids and mermen), Air = Sylphs. For Greco-Romans they are the four winds, and for Ceremonials they are the four Archangels.

Esbat: A Witches' gathering that is not on a Sabbat, usually occurring on a full or dark moon.

Ether (AKA Aether): An intangible material substance as opposed to a spiritual substance. It often refers to an unseen vaporous substance, as well as the occult counterpart of an atmosphere. Sometimes called 'Spirit'.

Etheric: Composed of Ether.

Evocation: Calling up spirits. (Not an invocation).

Familiar: An animal with psychic or Magickal abilities that is used by a Witch to aid them in their Magickal Workings.

Geomancy: The art of reading the Earth's energy and aligning yourself and your works to take best advantage of it.

Grimoire: A workbook containing ritual formulae, information and magickal properties of natural objects, and preparation of ritual equipment. Some people call their spell, ritual and magical information books 'Books of Shadows' and the herbal information a 'herbal Grimore'. Other people call the whole lot a Book of Shadows, or the whole lot a Grimoire. Still others, reserve the Grimoire for special Magickal techniques and personal Rituals not to be shared with others.

Grounding: Clearing and releasing excess energy. To focus back into the physical after Magickal and psychic workings.

Guardians: Another name for the Elementals.

Handfasting: A pagan wedding. Couples are Handfasted together for a specified number of days/years. (Usually a year and a day.) After which a handparting may take place if they wish to part or they may do another handfasting for another period of time. Some people have a registered marriage celebrant perform the Handfasting so that it will be a legally binding marriage in the eyes of the law. In modern practice, it is also used as a primary and permanent marriage when performed by registered Clergy at the request of the celebrants.

Handparting: A pagan form of divorce. The couple who had been Handfasted are now released. This is not a legal means of divorce if the Handfasting is of the legal and binding nature.

HPS: Shortened version of High Priestess. The female leader of a coven.

HP: The shortened version of High Priest. The male leader of a coven.

Intent: Your goal or purpose. You focus on this before doing a spell or ritual, in the hope of making it happen.

Invocation: An appeal or petition to a higher power. A prayer. Invocation is a method of establishing conscious ties with those aspects of the Goddess and God that dwells within us. To invoke.

Joss Stick: Incense in a stick form.

Karma: Divine justice. For every action there is a reaction. A good action will bring good, a bad one will bring bad.

Labrys: A double headed axe. A symbol of the Goddess.

Malleus Maleficarum: 'The Witches' Hammer' or 'Hammer for Witches'. A document used in the Witch trials, containing sections on how to test if a victim was a Witch and torture methods.

Megalith: A huge stone structure or monument. Stonehenge is the best known example of this.

Neo-Pagan: 'New Pagan'. Paganism is a religion (see below) of which Wicca belongs. All Wiccans are Pagan, but not all Pagans are Wiccan. The modern form of Paganism.

Pagan: Latin for 'A country dweller'. According to the dictionary, it is used to describe any religion that isn't Christian, Muslim or Jewish based (Abrahamic belief or Mosaic belief). Wicca is a form of Paganism, as is Shamanism, Druidism, etc. Some say that Paganism means 'nature-worshipping religion'.

Pantheon: A grouping of deities associated with a particular culture or time.

Patron Deity: A particular Goddess or God you feel most comfortable working with.

Pentacle: A five-pointed star surrounded by a circle. Also: A circular piece of wood, metal, clay or other material onto which a pentagram had been inscribed. It represents the element of Earth, also seen in the Tarot decks. Some people call the upside down pentagram a pentagram and the right way up one a pentacle, and some call them all pentacles. Items are placed on the pentacle during a ritual to consecrate them.

Pentagram: A five-pointed star. Each point represents an element: Earth, Air, Fire, Water and the fifth element, Ether or Spirit. It is the symbol of the horned God when turned upside down (nose, ears and horns make up the points). It is not the symbol of Satanism, as some believe. It is a symbol of protection, and many Wiccans and Pagans wear one as a symbol of their religion and for protection. (It was also used in Christianity as a protective amulet until the advent of modern evangelical Christianity). It can be inscribed into or drawn on objects to protect them. The upside down (inverted) version is a 'banishing' pentagram, and the right way up, the 'invoking' pentagram. The pentagram was used by many religions (including Christians) as a symbol of truth and protection before it was said to symbolize evil. The symbol apparently was used until the Inquisition as a positive symbol, and then its meaning was reversed. Some say that the upright pentagram shows Spirit/Divinity being first, it comes above everything else, and that the inverted pentagram shows Divinity at the bottom, and thus placed after everything else. This is said to be why Satanists use the inverted symbol, not because of its associations with the devil.

Poppet: (No I didn't spell it wrong... not puppet.) A doll used to represent a person. It is used in healing spells, love spells, hexes (although pins ARE NOT poked into it, that is Voodoo) etc. It can be wrapped in a ribbon or similar in a binding spell; it may be tied to another poppet for a love-binding spell. There are different uses for poppets in different spells. They can be made from cloth, wax, clay, etc.

Projective Hand: The hand you use for manual activities. The right hand in most people. This is the hand that gives out energy. It is opposite to the receptive hand, which receives energy.

Psychism: The act of being consciously psychic. When your conscious mind and your psychic mind are linked in perfect harmony.

Psychometry: Divination by holding an object belonging to another person.

Quabala: (Also spelled Kabala, Quabalah, Cabalah, Kabalah). An ancient Jewish system for spiritual knowledge. Often used in ceremonial Magick.

Receptive Hand: In a right-handed person this is the left hand. It is the hand through which energy is received.

Rede: 'To advise or counsel'. The Wiccan Rede is a passage of advice for Wiccans.

Sabbat: One of the eight festivals in the Pagan year. There are two solstice celebrations, two Equinox celebrations and some celebrations to mark season changes. Samhain, Litha, Lammas, Yule, Beltane, Imbolc, Mabon, Ostara. The four grand/major Sabbats are feminine Sabbats – Samhain, Imbolc, Beltane, and Lughnasadh. The four lesser Sabbats are masculine Sabbats – the Solstices and Equinoxes. (I don't think of them as being lesser and greater though).

Scry: To gaze at or into an object. Commonly this uses a crystal ball, bowl of water, mirror or a candle flame. (Called Scrying).

Scourge: A scourge is a whip, used in rituals by 'traditional' witches (being those who practice Gardnerian or Alexandrian Wicca, or variants of those forms of Wicca). It is not used much (if at all) today. I have never seen or heard of anyone actually having one, much less using one.

Shaman: Someone who obtains their contact with divinity and the earth through the use of substances which induce altered states of consciousness.

Sigil: A magickal symbol placed on an object as a seal.

Skyclad: 'Clad only in the sky'. Ritual nudity. Some people include not wearing jewelry, hair adornments and make-up as being skyclad. Many people believe that when you perform rituals naked you are free from restrictions and falsehood. Some say magick is more powerful when performed in this way.

Sympathetic Magick: Based on the principle that 'like cures like'. Most spells are done this way. Items that have similar qualities can be used to affect each other, i.e. plants are green – if growing plants are green, green candles therefore symbolize growth. You use a symbolic representation of the intent and whatever you do to it will be reflected on the actual goal. Poppets are sympathetic magick.

Talisman: An object Magically charged to attract something (e.g. money). A talisman is different to an amulet.

Thaumaturgy: Magick done for practical reasons. Magick to obtain things such as healing, money, etc.

Theurgy: Magick to evolve spiritually.

Thurible: An incense holder that is suspended from a chain that allows you to gently swing it to release the smoke.

Trilithon: A stone arch made from two upright slabs of rock or wood, with one lying atop. Commonly used as an altar.

Tuathail: 'Northward'. Means Widdershins.

Vibration: The rate at which energy moves. The slower the vibration, the denser the matter. The physical plane has a low vibration, and the Astral plane has a high vibration. As energy goes from a place of low vibration to a place of high vibration it produces heat, as it moves from a place of high vibration to one of low vibration it cools.

Visualization: Concentrating or imagining something very strongly as a visual image. The act of visualizing.

Widdershins: This is the opposite direction to Deosil. Counter-clockwise in the Northern Hemisphere and clockwise in the Southern Hemisphere.

Wiccaning: A pagan form of Christening. Unlike a Christening though, the child is placed in the care of the Goddess and God, not declared to be a Pagan. The child is free to choose whichever religion they like, but a Wiccaning is done to protect them until they are old enough to become Pagan themselves.

Cleansing and Preparing Altar Tools

Purification and dedication of your Wiccan ritual tools should be done as soon as you can after you get them.

Certainly purify them at least, before using or wearing the object!

Items that have a heavy, dark or hot energy need purification. This is particularly true of crystals. When clear, they will feel cool, tingly, bright, or positive.

A purified object is much more powerful than a contaminated one, and its magick is less likely to go awry.

Purification, dedication, and consecration of ritual objects take place in sacred space – that is, within ritual. So begin by casting a Circle. Before going further, check that the item won't be harmed first.

Water: Crystals and other stones may be damaged by hot water. Always use cool water. Some crystals (salt crystals for example) may be damaged even by cool water. Leather may harden in water. Fabric may run, fade, or shrink – especially in hot water.

Sunlight: Gem stones, crystals, and other items may also be damaged – faded, melted, or broken – by heat.

Salt: Opals, metal, leather, and fabric can be damaged by salt, either dry or in water.

Smudging or Flame: Stones may be damaged by heat. Other items, like cloth and plant material, may be flammable – use extreme care.

Moon Bath: The simplest way to purify Wiccan tools is to bathe them in moonlight. This will not only cleanse them, but recharge them as well.

Except for the very lightest cleansing, you'll probably need to leave them for at least one full cycle of the moon. Full to full, or dark to dark – whichever feels right to you. For lighter moon-washes, use the waning moonlight.

If your altar is in the moonlight, this is the best place to leave your ritual tools for a moon bath. Otherwise, hanging them in a tree is good. (If it's sparkly and you have lots of crows, ravens, or magpies around though, they might make off with it when you're not looking!)

Herb Baths: You can bury your Wiccan tools in herbs for cleansing. Particularly effective are rose petals, sage, and mint. This is a lovely way to clean sacred objects, but it can take a while.

Sea Salt: A faster method is a sea salt bath. You can bury your Wiccan tools in dry sea salt, or a salt-water bath. Washing it in the ocean, or even running wild water like a river, is even better. If it feels like it needs a very deep cleansing, you can leave it in the salt water for a period of time – even in the moonlight, for a double whammy.

Earth Cleansing: You can bury certain items in Earth for purification – like stones and crystals. This will do a very deep cleansing. Simply bury them, pointing downward, into Earth outdoors, between the roots of a tree is ideal. If you can't manage that, bury them with a potted plant. The real trick to this method of purification is remembering exactly where you buried your ritual tools! Be sure to leave a marker that is unlikely to be removed.

Smudging: Even more rapid is smudging, particularly using cedar or sage. Pass the ritual tools through the smoke a few times. This is enough for most purposes. But you can do as much as you need. This is a great method for healing tools, especially stones.

Bathing in Light: Similar to smudging, you can pass ritual tools through (or above) the flame of your Goddess candle. The light will purify and remove any negative energies. It needs to be done carefully, to avoid burning yourself and scorching your tools.

Cleansing Breath: After coming to a place of calm and peace, you can blow into your ritual tools with the intention of being a conduit for Divine energy. Blow the negativity away, and blow positivity in – imagining this as white or golden light replacing any shadows in the object.

Running Water: Holding your ritual tools under cold running water can cleanse them, but this is usually unadvisable except for stones. In which case, if they are pointed, make sure the points face downward with the flow of water, so the negative energy flows out and away. You can do this with tap water as a last resort, but living water is much better.

Dedication of Ritual Tools

The dedication, or programming, of Wiccan tools is simply setting an intention for their use; and communicating that intention to the ritual item, making sure that you have its consent.

- This cup will be my Chalice.
- This knife will be my Athame.
- This shell will be for healing.
- This stone will be for grounding energies.
- And so on...

The dedication of your Wiccan tools begins in those first moments when you scan to find the right tools for you.

It continues when you pick up the items, and ask them whether they are willing to work with you, and in what way.

The purpose of dedication is to have the two of you – you and the Wiccan tool – coordinating your energies and focusing them on a single purpose. This magnifies the power available to you.

How to Dedicate Your Ritual Tools

Once you've purified your Wiccan tools, take a minute or two in sacred space, that is, still within the Ritual Circle to quietly feel the item's energy.

Once you have a sense of that, visualize clearly what purpose you have chosen it for. Send that image or idea into the ritual item. Ask it if it is willing to participate in this.

Then sit quietly and open yourself to hearing its response. You may feel an increase in energy – which signifies yes, or a decrease – which means no.

Chances are that at this stage, the objects will be right on board. If so, this step serves to clarify the item's purpose.

If the Object Disagrees

It is possible that it rejects the idea, even now. If so, there are three likely reasons:

- It has not been sufficiently cleansed. In this case, do a deep purification.
- Your intention is not clear, or in some way harmful. In this case, spend some time exploring your intention and getting clear on what you want to do – and why. Divination might help, since it is excellent at revealing hidden currents.
- It has a specific purpose in coming to you, but not the one you thought. In this case, spend some time with this item, and ask it to reveal its purpose to you. Sooner or later – generally as soon as you're willing to hear it – you'll understand. At which point you can dedicate the object and yourself to that intention.

Consecration of Sacred Objects

For some items, dedication may be enough. Personally, I think you can never go wrong by invoking the Divine.

Consecrating your ritual tools is a way of setting them at a high vibration level. This protects them from contamination by negative energy, and charges them with Divine energy. This greatly increases the item's power.

Consecration is especially useful for anything that may be used in healings.

You may want to consecrate your ritual tools to specific deities. For instance, Tara or Quan Yin for compassion, Kali for releasing the old, Hecate for protection, Artemis for clear focus, etc. Or you may simply align each item with positive energy.

How to Consecrate Sacred Objects

After purification and dedication, you can do one of the following in sacred space, using both your imagination to visualize it and your voice to ask for it:

- Hold the item in your dominant hand (usually the right), and focus on the purest, brightest white light you can imagine. Imagine it filling yourself, your sacred space, and the ritual object.
- Smudge the Wiccan tool with cedar smoke, visualizing the sacred power of the cedar aligning its energy with the Most High.
- Pass the object 'through' (or above) the light of your Goddess candle (or, if you choose, both Goddess and God candles). Think of that light penetrating and filling all the spaces between the atoms in your Wiccan tool.

After each of these, place your Wiccan tool on your object, in the very center. Focusing on it completely, ask your Deities to sanctify this tool.

State clearly, 'Only the most pure Divine energy may enter and work through this sacred object.'

Hold this intent, until you feel it has completely 'taken'. Then close your intent with, 'So mote it be! Blessed be.'

Your Wiccan tool is now consecrated.

Charging Your Ritual Tools With Magickal Energy

You can do this the same way you consecrated, essentially. The difference is that you build up a certain Magickal energy beforehand, in Ritual space, and then fill the Wiccan tool with that energy.

In this case, you can use a smudging herb that contains that energy.

You might want to use essential oils to instill certain energies into your Wiccan tools. They can be dabbed onto the object. But be sure it won't damage the material.

Another option is to place your ritual tools on the altar during rituals and spell-casting. This is especially popular – and practical – to do at group rituals, when appropriate. Lots of good Magickal power can be raised, and if you've set the intention, the object can soak it up.

Practice Techniques:
Grounding and Centering

Technique 1

Sit peacefully and relax in a wooden chair or on the ground, outside (the latter is usually the most effective). Place a lit candle (white) in front of you to focus on. Let the ground or chair support you. Let your muscles go. You don't have to exert any effort to sit there. Take in an easy, deep breath... and let it out of your mouth, parting your lips slightly as you exhale. Let your arms feel heavy, pulling down your shoulders. Breathe... Let that heavy feeling flow down your torso and legs, so you feel heavy and relaxed all the way down to your feet on the ground.

Now you are connected to the Earth Power, and the Sky Power; feel them join together in a balance in your center, and in your Self. You are grounded now in all things, and may journey deeper in to other realms. This is the beginning of a meditative state, the state in which the mind is ready for both magickal work and ritual.

Picture and feel roots growing from your feet down into the ground. Just like a tree's roots... going down into the layers of cool dirt... growing around rocks... traveling further and further down into the earth. Let the roots grow as deeply as you wish.

Now feel the healing, rhythmic energy of the earth itself flowing up through your roots... slowly traveling up... through your roots, up to your feet and quickly filling your entire body. Feel this positive, grounded, earth energy throughout your being. Take in a deep, cleansing breath... and release.

When you are ready, open your eyes and know that this grounded energy will remain with you throughout your day.

Technique 2

Centering: Close your eyes, and place your feet firmly on the ground or floor. Gather all the energy in your body to a nice round glowing ball in what you feel is the center of your body. This is centering. Find a center point in yourself and feel it there, steady and calm. If you are only centering and not moving on to grounding, maintain this as long as you need to until you feel you have centered yourself enough.

Grounding: Center yourself first. Breathe deeply. As you breathe in, feel the clean, fresh air filling your whole body, filling your Self. As you breathe slowly out, feel the worries and problems of your everyday life, your mundane existence, dropping away, through your feet into the earth. Now imagine that ball slowly putting down a thick taproot, small at first, getting thicker, through the base of your spine, down into your feet. Feel that root get thicker as it goes down through layers of soil and rock, pushing deep into the earth.

Imagine the water table under all those layers of earth, and when your root reaches the water, draw the cool, fresh energy of the earth flow up to your centered energy ball and blend with it – the Earth Power is a deep well, and you are drawing it up into yourself, through your Chakras, up your spine and through the top of your head. Feel the Earth Power fill you, rise through you like refreshing water, and feel it flow through your center, constantly providing both new energy and a route for negative and unhealthy energy to flow away, carried by the Earth Power back to the depths of the living well to be cleansed and made useful again.

As the energy flows through the top of your head, feel it branch out, spreading like the arms of a tree. Feel it grow to the sky, into the stars, and touch the bright Sky Power pulsing overhead. As it pulses, draw it down through your branches, down through those arms and into your center, to connect with your center, to join there in union and balance with the Earth Power. Feel the cool breezes of the Sky Power invigorate and cleanse you, bringing inspiration and joy from the vast Universe into your center.

Phase Two

Continuing Along the Path

Magic is not a practice. It is a living, breathing web of energy that, with our permission, can encase our every action.

Dorothy Morrison, *Everyday Magic*

As you continue along the Path to Priesthood, you will find the road has a few more obstacles. As you make your way, pause to reflect on what you find here, some of those rocks littering the path hide gems that can take you to many places. If you look closely, there is much here to make you a wiser Cleric, tools that you may pass along to those wishing to learn. Heed well, you first must commit much to mind and heart before becoming an effective teacher.

Color

Color affects all things in different ways; it can greatly affect the Magickal properties of things. What would be a calming color in one item, can have a much different effect on another. Combining two incompatible colors can have disastrous results.

Even the so-called 'normal' world has learned that colors affect people in very definite ways. Offices choose specific colors designed to increase productivity. Hospitals use colors that aid in healing. Prisons utilize colors to have a calming effect. The list goes on and on.

Color Chart

The color used in a candle will greatly influence what it can do when used in Ritual or Magick. Bear this in mind when choosing a candle for whatever your intent is based upon. Doing so will allow for greater success in your endeavor.

Following is a list of colors and their meaning. It will assist you in choosing wisely and should be paid close attention to. Some colors are complementary in nature and can be used well together, while others, when combined, negate each other. The meanings found in the color chart will help you to avoid this issue.

Amber: Develop witchery skills.
Black: Endings, closing of doors, psychic work, death, ward off negativity, remove hexes, protection, spirit contact, truth, night, reversing, releasing, repel dark magic and negative thought forms, and remove discord or confusion.
Copper: Passion, money goals, professional growth, fertility in business, career maneuvers.
Dark Blue: The Goddess (representative ritual candle), Water Elemental, truth, inspiration, dreams, protection, psychism, change, deep emotion, peace, meditation, impulse, and West.

Light Blue: Psychic awareness, intuition, opportunity, understanding, quests, safe journeys, patience, tranquility, ward depression, healing, happiness, harmony in the home, and peace.

Blue (any): Health.

Brown: Earth Elemental, endurance, animal health, steadiness, houses and homes, physical objects, overcoming uncertainty and hesitancy, attract money and financial success, concentration, ESP, intuition, study.

Gold: The God, solar energy, physical strength, power, success, mental growth, skill sought, healing energy, fortune, divination, creative work, intuition, money, fast luck, attracts higher influences.

Gray: Non-nature-type fairy magic such as communication with the fairy realms, travel to the Otherworld, vision quests, veiling, cancellation, hesitation, neutrality, and competition.

Green: Lord and Lady of Greenwood, Earth Elemental, herb magic, nature-type fairy magic (such as blessing a garden), luck, fertility, healing, balance, employment, prosperity, courage, agriculture, changing direction or attitudes, North, money, growth, abundance, generosity, renewal, and marriage. *Warning: Do not use with anyone who has cancer.*

Green / Yellow: Negate discord, sickness, anger, and jealousy.

Indigo: Meditations, spirit communication, karma workings, learn the ancient wisdom; neutralize another's magic, and ward against slander, lies or undesirable competition.

Lavender: Spiritual development, psychic growth, divination, sensitivity to the Otherworld, blessings.

Magenta: Very high vibration frequency that tends to work fast so usually burned with other candles, quick change, spiritual healing, and exorcism.

Orange: The God (representative candle), strength, healing, pulling things to you, adaptability, luck, vitality, encouragement, attraction, stimulation, energy, clearing the mind, dominance, sudden changes, and change of luck.

Pink: Honor, morality, friendships, emotional love, peace, femininity, affection, romance, spiritual awakening, healing of the spirit, togetherness.

Purple: Power, dignity, spiritual development, meditation, spirituality, intuition, ambition, spirit communication, tension, business progress, healing severe diseases, occult wisdom, success, idealism, higher psychic ability, break bad luck, drive away evil, honors.

Red: Fire Elemental, strength, power, blood of the moon, lust, love, survival, energy, health, vigor, enthusiasm, courage, passion, sexuality.

Silver: The Goddess, lunar magic, telepathy, intuition, dreams, meditation, psychic development, female power, communication, success, balance, ward negativity.

Violet: Self-improvement, intuition, success in searches, and creative work.

White: The Lady and Lord together, the Goddess, virginity (the true meaning, not sexually), full moon magic, purity, protection, truth, meditation, peace, sincerity, justice, warding off doubt and fear.

Yellow: Air Elemental, the moon, accelerated learning, memory, breaking mental blocks, divination, clairvoyance, mental alertness, intellectual growth, prosperity, learning, changes, harmony, creativity.

Herbs and Plants

Herbs and plants have, for centuries, been used in both Magick and healing. Even modern medicine finds its medicinal roots in the healing herbs of time gone by. Many can be made into a tea for drinking, others placed in medicine or spirit bags, the uses go on and on. Although the following list is lengthy, we will only touch on the Magickal or medicinal qualities of some of the many plants and herbs. Many different cultures use plants and herbs in their spiritual paths. These have been included to widen your knowledge and understanding. We hope this will spur you to investigate further into the realms of herbology.

Acacia

Acacia, a native of Africa; with many subspecies found around the world (including North America) is also known as Gum Arabic and is found as a shrub or tree. It flowers in elongated groups. The leaves point outwardly from stem.

From December to June the Acacia exudes a gum-like sap. This is what is used in both medicine and Magick. The gum should be mixed into a mucilage as follows: Gum Arabic is usually dissolved in water to make a mucilage.

Mucilage: A dose is from 1 to 4 tsp.

Syrup: Mix 1 part mucilage with 3 parts of syrup. A dose is from 1-4 tsp.

In medicine, it has been used to sooth respiratory ailments and has been used in a sweetened form to treat typhoid fever.

Its Magickal properties are spirituality and purification.

Agrimony

Agrimony is a perennial, herbaceous plant found in grassy areas. It bears yellow flowers that have a scent resembling Apricot. The flowers turn into rust-red berries. A member of the rose family, it blooms from June until early September.

It is found in the temperate climates of the Northern Hemisphere and therefore is fairly common to North America.

Agrimony has long been used to cure a variety of ailments from healing wounds to intestinal and eye conditions. It was at one time called 'all cure' by early doctors.

Its Magickal properties are psychic healing and protection.

It is said that when carried in a medicine bag, it will protect the bearer and return negative spells to the sender. It is also a useful smudge for cleansing the aura.

Allspice

Allspice is a plant native to the warmer regions such as Southern Mexico, South America and the Greater Antilles. In North America, it is usually found in both the full berry form and ground form in supermarkets' spice sections.

Allspice is burned as an incense to attract money or luck, and is also added to incense mixtures. It is also commonly used to promote healing.

Aloe

The Aloe Vera is a medicinal plant, which used properly, can be the best treatment for sunburn and other minor burns. It is found predominantly in hotter climates such as South America, but is also found in some southern parts of Northern America.

The part of the Aloe Vera used, is the leaves. The Aloe is an emollient, purgative and vulnerary. It is also used for its antibacterial, anesthetic and antiseptic properties, and is good to use as a tool for restoration of tissue. It is most commonly used on burns and minor cuts, and, as mentioned earlier, is especially good for sunburn. Aloe is very useful on rashes caused by Poison Ivy.

The magickal uses of Aloe are not easily located. It is a feminine plant, and its planet is the moon. Its element is water, and its powers are protection and luck. Aloe can be hung over the home for good luck. Carry it with you to protect yourself against evil, or to protect yourself from clumsiness.

Warnings: Do not ingest if you are pregnant, Aloe may cause uterine contractions.

Angelica Root (Dong Quai)

Angelica Root grows predominantly in the colder Northern regions and is found in its wild state in Finland, Norway, Denmark, Greenland and Iceland.

This plant can usually be found in herbal stores under the name of Dong Quai.

It is used in exorcism, protection, visions and healing.

Star Anise

Star Anise is native to the Eastern United States, but many sub-varieties are found in the Asian regions of the world (primarily in four provinces of China, where it is grown commercially).

Used in medicine as an antibacterial, antioxidant and natural insecticide, it also seems to have certain sedative qualities.

Magickally, it is used for purification and is said to enhance psychic ability.

Basil

Basil is native to India, but is easily grown in almost any region, as long as you provide warmth. It is very sensitive to cold and will not thrive under those conditions. Quite common as a cooking herb, it is used extensively in Italian and Asian cuisine.

Basil has strong antioxidant properties and has been used in Siddha (the traditional medicine practice of India) for asthma, stress and diabetes.

In magickal practice it is used for attracting love, providing protection and wealth.

Benzoin Gum

Benzoin Gum is the resin from the Styrax Tree, which is native to Sumatra, Thailand and Java.

It has antibiotic and disinfectant qualities that have long been used in Islamic medicine.

When burned as incense it is useful in grounding and stabilizing.

Bergamot

Bergamot is almost exclusively native to the coastal region of Calabria, Italy. The oils are used most commonly and can be readily found in herbal supply stores.

The oil has been used for both neurological and blood disorders successfully. It has also been used in the treatment of cystic fibrosis.

It is said that Bergamot will aid in increasing the user's creativity and luck.

Black Cohosh

Black Cohosh is an herb that acts very similar to the female-produced chemical estrogen. It is becoming more popular as people are learning more about it. It has an enormous number of medicinal uses and has been used by hundreds of years by Native American Indians.

The medicinal part of Black Cohosh that is used is the root. It is considered an astringent, emmenagogue, expectorant, diuretic, sedative, and an antispasmodic. The roots can be boiled and ingested; this helps to treat fatigue, sore throats, arthritis, and rattlesnake bites. It has estrogenic effects, and has been prescribed to women going through menopause. It is said to calm the nervous system and stimulate the heart and it reduces blood pressure because it is an excellent herb to open restricted blood vessels.

A surprising magickal fact about Black Cohosh is that it is

considered masculine. This is surprising because the herb is associated so much with the female hormone, estrogen. Its magical powers include love, courage, protection and potency. Men should carry it with them to help with impotency, and anyone can carry it to invoke a feeling of courage.

Warning: Some reports have stated that large quantities can cause symptoms similar to poisoning. Black Cohosh has estrogenic effects, if you have been advised not to take birth control pills, be wary of Black Cohosh. Because of its estrogenic effects, pregnant women should avoid it. Do not use if you have heart disease.

Blue Cohosh Root
This plant has been used as a medicinal herb by Native Americans. European midwives found that when combined with other specific herbs it could be used as a contraceptive agent.

It is quite common in Eastern U.S. hardwood forests.

It is used in many Pagan homes as a home blessing.

Dragon's Blood Resin
This tree is native to the Canary Islands, Azores and Morocco. It is not a true tree, but an herbaceous plant. Due to its growth pattern it is often mistaken for a tree.

The reddish resin is commonly used as a dye and is the original coloring agent for the Stradivarius violin.

The resin has also been used for medicinal purposes. However, due to the technical nature of the available information; we will not pursue this area.

It is often burned as an incense to provide both protection and power.

Echinacea
Echinacea (commonly known as Cone Flower) is one of the herbs more commonly in use in Western civilization today. It is used

extensively to prevent and treat the common cold as well as many other viruses and bacterial infections. Many people ingest it commonly throughout the cold and flu seasons in order to have an herbal shield against rampaging germs.

Echinacea is used frequently as an antibiotic, antiseptic, immune stimulator, depurative, digestive and a blood purifier. It helps to stimulate proper digestion, and as a mouthwash, it can be used for the treatment of painful gums and toothaches. An infusion can be made of the herb which can help to aid in arthritis pain and tonsillitis. Apply Echinacea to burns and wounds on the skin to promote quicker tissue recovery and healing. It also helps to stimulate the body's cells to produce a chemical that is naturally produced by the white blood cells while fighting infection. This chemical is called interferon. The medicinal part of the plant is the rootstock.

Echinacea is often used in spells to strengthen their power, just as the herb is used to strengthen the immune system. It was used by the Native Americans not only to strengthen their spells, but as a precious offering to spirits.

Echinacea prefers dry and open areas; it is a perennial North American native plant. Spread out the seeds without pushing them into the soil and keep watered. It grows best in full sun, and the best time to pull the roots and harvest the plant is in autumn. Echinacea has a natural odor; if it is not present do not use it.

Warning: Echinacea can cause a tingling sensation in the mouth when ingested, but this is natural and dissipates after a few minutes. Echinacea is listed with the FDA as 'undefined safety' due to the fact that no one has ever had a toxic reaction to the herb.

Eucalyptus

Eucalyptus is native to Eastern Australia and is usually found in its sub-alpine areas.

The oil from the Eucalyptus is often used as a cleaning agent as well as an ingredient in many cough suppressants. It is also an active ingredient in many insect repellants.

It has been introduced to many countries around the world and is now considered an invasive plant in many areas because of its tendency to lower the water table due to the massive requirement for liquid; it also has no natural controls outside its native soil and the tree produces natural, highly combustible oil. This oil has been found to ignite at very low temperatures and can be extremely explosive in nature.

Pagans often associate it with purification rituals.

Fennel Seeds

Fennel is one of the nine plants invoked in the Anglo-Saxon nine herbs charm. The plant can be found growing wild throughout North America, Canada, Asia and Australia.

Although it is used primarily as a cooking herb, it has many medicinal uses. Some of these uses are for intestinal, eye and blood disorders.

The most powerful of its many Magickal attributes seem to be protection and healing.

Fenugreek Seeds

The exact history of Fenugreek is somewhat sketchy. However, it is thought that it originated in very early Iraq or Egypt. Both areas have carbon-dated samples that have been determined to be from the Bronze Age.

The plant (seeds, mainly) have been shown to be helpful with arthritis as well as being capable of increasing libido. It is also widely used to assist in the increased production of breast milk.

Ingesting the seeds or using them in cooking is said to elevate wisdom and success.

Feverfew

Native to the Balkan Peninsula, this plant has been introduced around the world and is readily available in North America.

As its name implies, it is a very effective herbal fever reducer and is often used to relieve headaches as well.

It is often used in healing and purification Ritual.

Warnings: Long-term use of Feverfew for headaches has been known to cause 'rebound headaches', muscle and joint pain. It should also never be used by women who are pregnant or those using blood thinning agents because it has been known to increase the risk of bleeding.

Frankincense Resin

Frankincense is a resin that comes from the Boswellia tree, which is native to the Arabian Peninsula and Northern Africa.

This resin has been used as a treatment for arthritis and in the healing of wounds. This has been a primarily Ayurvedic medicine practice.

It is burned as an incense to provide protection, increased spirituality and cleansing of negative energies.

Galangal Root

This is native to South East Asia and Thailand, where it is used in various soups and curries.

It has long been used as a curative for skin infections such as ringworm and eczema.

Galangal Root is known to have been used in early African-American folk medicine.

It is used for protection and energy in many Pagan paths.

Ginger Root

Ginger root is traditionally used in cooking and as a food source, but it has a natural intestinal calmative and is frequently used as an anti-nausea agent. It is quite effective when used for motion sickness, morning sickness and to lessen the nausea associated with chemotherapy.

It carries Magickal aspects related to strength, courage and health.

Gingko

Gingko is an extremely ancient plant with fossil specimens found to be some two hundred and seventy thousand years old. These specimens have been discovered in both the Northern and Southern Hemispheres of the planet, so an exact location of origin is difficult to pinpoint. Currently, it is found primarily in Eastern China, where it grows wild. It is cultivated in North America, but attempts to naturalize it have been less than successful.

It is highly regarded by Buddhists due to its long life and effect on the memory, and can often be found planted in and around Buddhist temples.

Gingko has long been used to improve memory and this is a returning trend. It has been shown that it has been effective to treat dementia patients, but seems to have no ability to improve the condition of those suffering from Alzheimer's.

In folk and Magickal use it helps improve intelligence and energy.

Warnings: Gingko is known to act as an anti-coagulant and should never be used by anyone using a blood thinning agent such as Warfarin or Coumadin.

Hyssop

A native of the Mediterranean and Central Asia, this herb is widely cultivated throughout the world.

It has been used by a great many religious paths as a tool of purification; it is used as the filler of the aspergillum in the Catholic Church for the purification of both a space and the congregation. In the Christian Bible it is mentioned by name,

'Thou shalt purge me with Hyssop, and I shall be clean'; Psalm 51:7.
It has few medicinal uses and caution should be taken when using it. Hyssop is also a good border plant for herb gardens because of its natural insect repellant nature. A study showed it has caused fatal convulsions in rats.

Planted in a garden or around the yard, it provides protection from negative energy.

Jasmine Flowers

Jasmine grows primarily in tropical and sub-tropical regions of Africa, Asia and Europe.

The plant is cultivated and used in homes throughout India for worship and is commonly worn as a hair ornament by the females of a household. It is also frequently used during wedding ceremonies to promote both love and peace in the family.

Juniper Berries

Many species of Juniper thrive throughout the world. In North America, Scandinavia and Northern Europe, a number of the species are used in foods, most notably as a means to minimize the 'gaminess' of wild meats.

During times of famine, many Native American tribes have used Juniper Berries as an appetite suppressant. It is from this practice that research has started for its effectiveness in the treatment of diabetes (the appetite suppressant quality has been associated with the release of insulin from the pancreas).

The berries have long been associated with increased stamina and strength.

Lemon Verbena

This plant is native to most of South America. Its flowers are used for rites of purification and love. It is considered a mild antioxidant and has some, though limited, medicinal qualities.

Lemongrass

Native to both India and Tropical Asia, Lemongrass is a common herb used in cooking.

When brewed as a tea, lemongrass is effective in relieving anxiety and is also used extensively in Ayurvedic medicine to relieve coughs and nasal congestion.

Its Magickal use is primarily focused on purification and clearing.

Licorice Root

Originating in Southern Europe and portions of Asia, it is a popular flavor in some sweets.

Licorice Root is used in traditional Chinese medicine to relieve spasmodic coughing and has been found effective in both homeopathic and conventional medicine to relieve ulcerations of the mouth and peptic ulcers.

It is used in Pagan paths to improve eloquence, humor and healing.

Warnings: Excessive use of Licorice Root is known to be toxic to both the liver and cardiovascular system and can cause hypertension and edema.

Lobelia

There is a wide variety of Lobelia species throughout the world.

Native Americans used the plant to treat muscular and respiratory disorders. In China, it is listed as one of the fifty fundamental herbs in traditional medicine.

Warnings: Due to its similarities to Tobacco, it should only be administered by a qualified practitioner.

Oak Moss

This lichen is found commonly throughout the mountainous regions of the Northern Hemisphere. It can be similar in appearance to Spanish Moss, but is unrelated.

Oak Moss has been used medicinally for over one thousand years and is considered a powerful antibiotic.

Placing it on your Altar or around your home promotes grounding and peace.

Nettle

Nettle is widely distributed and is native to North America, Europe, Asia and Africa. The most common variety is the Stinging Nettle.

Most of its medicinal use is found in folk medicine. The plant has been used in the treatment of arthritis, when brewed into a tea. Nettle was used for the treatment of nausea, asthma, hypertension and urinary tract infections to name but a few.

The active portion of the plant is found in the stinging leaves. This contains formic acid, histamine and serotonin.

Although the stinging sensation can be painful, it is rarely harmful with the exception of the New Zealand variety, which has been attributed to the death of some livestock and possibly one known human death.

Patchouli

Patchouli is native virtually throughout Asia as well as India and West Africa.

In Japan and Malaysia it is often used as a treatment for venomous snake bites; in China it is used to treat headaches and nausea.

The oil is a potent insect repellant and frequently used much as Americans use Aromatic Cedar to keep moths out of cloth.

Burned as incense, it is said to aid in protection from psychic and negative energies, elevate libido and draw wealth.

Pennyroyal

Pennyroyal is quite common to North America and Europe. The fresh or dried leaves have been used to treat colds, influenza and have been used to treat smallpox. The flowers are believed to increase strength, power and protection.

Warnings: Care must be used if handling pennyroyal oil as it is very toxic.

Pennyroyal should not be used by anyone who is pregnant or plans to become pregnant in the near future. It has been known to cause spontaneous abortion (miscarriage).

Peppermint: Peppermint is a hybrid of the mint family that is considered a native of England.

It is known to alleviate insomnia and is also used in soaps and shampoos and acts as a natural cooling agent. It is used as an aid to irritable bowel syndrome.

In ritual and spell practice it is said to draw wealth, health and intuition.

Rosehips Seeds

These fruits are very high in vitamin C and contain trace amounts of vitamins A and B as well as being a good source of the antioxidant Lycopene. They are used to prevent colds and influenza.

Magickally they are used to provide protection and wealth.

Rosemary

This is a common herb used in cooking. In medicine, it has been proven to improve memory.

In the Middle Ages, Rosemary was used in wedding ceremonies to ensure lasting love.

Magickal practices, uses for Rosemary include protecting, purifying and as a divinatory tool.

Sage, Clary

Clary Sage is used as a smudging agent for purification and home blessings. *Culpeper's Complete Herbal* states that a sage seed placed in the eye of someone who has a foreign object in it would draw the object out. It was called clear eye in that book.

Sage, White

Common throughout dry regions of North America, it was used as a food source by many Native American Tribes.

It was and is considered a powerful cleansing and purifying agent when used as a smudge stick.

St. John's Wort

St. John's Wort is native to virtually any temperate region throughout the world.

It has been proven through numerous medical studies to be an effective antidepressant, sometimes providing the same outcome as standard antidepressants. This plant has been called a 'cure all' in modern society, it is not. Many herbalists are using other plants that demonstrate the same characteristics because of this.

Native Americans have used it externally as an anti-inflammatory, astringent and antiseptic.

Pagan practices use it as an aid to purification and protection.

Sandalwood, Red

Red Sandalwood is found exclusively in Southern India, primarily in the Nepal area, and exporting of the wood is closely regulated. This wood is considered sacred in Hinduism and is frequently used in Ritual.

While it has no known medicinal uses, it is considered to provide the bearer with energy, courage and protection.

Sandalwood, White

This species of tree is native to India, Malaysia, Sri Lanka and most of the Indian sub-continent. It has been harvested to the point that the majority of wild growth has reached near extinction. Naturalized cultivars have been created and are the primary source of this sought-after product.

Like its relative the Red Sandalwood, it has few if any

medicinal uses, but is widely used in various religious practices. In incense form, it is used to raise spirituality and energy, it is also used for cleansing and purification.

Solomon's Seal Root

This plant flourishes around the world and is a popular border plant in many American gardens.

It has many of the same properties as Aloe; it is used to facilitate the healing of minor wounds and as a wash to help control acne.

The stems and roots are edible after proper treatment, but the berries are considered poisonous. Planting them in your garden is said to provide protection and increase spirituality.

Tansy

Tansy is native to all of mainland Europe. It has been used to treat intestinal worms, rheumatism, and digestive problems. Tansy is also a natural insect repellant and is often placed on windowsills to ward off flies and mosquitoes. Grown in the yard, it seems to ward off ants. Its presence increases connection with the Goddess during ritual or meditation.

Warnings: Do not confuse Tansy with Tansy Ragwort. Tansy Ragwort is quite toxic and should be avoided. They are quite similar in appearance. Learn the differences by sight before cultivating this plant.

Thyme

Thyme is a common herb that will grow, with proper care, in almost any region.

In medicine, Thyme has been used to dress bandages before the use of antibiotics. Brewed into a tea it can be used to calm coughs. It is still used as an ingredient in Listerine due to its mouth freshening abilities.

It is mostly burned as an incense for cleansing and clearing a sacred space.

Valerian Root

Little seems to be known of the Valerian plant's origin, but it was mentioned by Hippocrates and was used in medieval Sweden.

The root of the plant produces an effective sedative and is also an anticonvulsive and migraine treatment.

Ingested as a tea it aids in sleep, provides protection and has a purifying quality.

Witch Hazel

Its origin is commonly considered to be England. It has long been used for its astringent properties.

Witch Hazel is used for purification, to promote chastity and increase psychic ability.

Wormwood

Wormwood is a natural flea repellant and has long been used in some potent alcoholic beverages. It is the fastest of all malaria medicines and inhibits growth of bacteria.

In Magickal practice Wormwood is said to heighten psychic ability.

Yarrow

Yarrow is native throughout the Northern Hemisphere.

This plant has been known as a powerful healing herb for centuries. Achilles was said to have carried it into battle to heal his troops. This plant contains Salicylic Acid and is a good headache reliever.

Native Americans often chewed this 'life plant' to relieve toothaches or made into an infusion to calm earaches.

Its presence induces courage, love and power.

Its presence induces courage, love and power.

Crystals and Gemstones

Many stones and crystals are very important to the Goddess and God; they are a source of many powers. As you grow in the Craft, you will learn the full nature of all that is provided. Here is listed various minerals and crystals along with the most important properties of each. The act of carrying or placing one alone will have the desired effect.

The list of stones provided here is by no means complete. There are many thousands of various crystals, mineral and gemstones; each having their own personal Magickal qualities. This will give you a start and hopefully will provide you with an interest in researching more on the subject.

Agate

Chalcedony Quartz. Red, orange, yellow and browns; solid, grounding. For stomach, colon, liver, spleen, kidneys, X-ray/radiation.

Moss coloring: Draws new friends. Relieves exhaustion and heals problems with the neck and back. Money and happiness spells. Centering. Blood sugar, anorexia/food issues, lymph nodes. Balances emotions.

Iris pattern: Insight, restores nerve feeling and healing after injury/burns.

Picture pattern: Gaze into for meditation. Left/right brain balance; pineal, pituitary; coordination.

Blue Lace pattern: Patience, peace. Cools.

Crazy Lace pattern: Spiritual powers: aids with energy lows. Relieves emotional pain. Opens the way for laughter. Healing attributes: Strengthens the heart. Clears energy blockages. Brings vitality to major organs.

Flame pattern: Spiritual powers. Provides clarity during periods of transition. Stimulates awareness. Healing attributes:

Enhances physical vitality. Treatment of burns and relieving pain.

Amazonite

Receptive. Element: Earth. Solid light blue/turquoise. Gentle, friendly, calming, soothing. Opens throat, heart, and solar plexus centers for self-expression, artistic creativity, healing, throat, thyroid, nerve and brain paths. Reduces self-damaging behavior, increases straight posture for self-respect, confidence, grace, self-assuredness with communication. It works to provide clarity and insight. This works both for the confidence required of the good gambler and for the self-confidence building that leads to every success. Amazonite creates a feeling of power. It is the original 'you can get what you want if you want it bad enough stone'. It also leads one away from the self-destructive behavior that sometimes surfaces when we experience disappointments.

Amazonite is the stone that clearly leads one to understand that 'more is never enough'. Great for anyone in a 12-step program of any kind. All of us feel aggravation from time to time. Reach for your Amazonite and feel a surging of peace and calmness flow to your heart center. Amazonite also aligns the physical and astral bodies. Many times we feel out of sorts when these two bodies are not nested together. If you feel disconnected in the morning after awakening, sit for a minute with your Amazonite and visualize your two bodies coming together. Amazonite has been used to enhance communication between lovers, and as a general all-purpose healing stone for health maintenance. There is also a quality that appears to assist in reactivation of blocked neural passages. Good for pinched nerves, spinal difficulties and could be helpful for bursitis.

Calcite

Milky yellow, peach, green, white or clear crystals. Soft.
Red/pink: Receptive. Element: Water. Powers: Doubles the power

(all calcites double the power) of any energy directed to it. Also directs energy to specific points. Fosters spirituality, creates peace, sweeping action to balance and clear the Chakras. Used in love rituals, it is calming, centering and grounding. Releases negative emotions. Aids feeling protected emotionally. Eliminates stress, reduces hypertension, brings rejuvenation and revitalization to the entire body and works with the circulatory system.

Green: Receptive. Element: Earth. Tranquility; soothes the spiritual heart; helps us learn from lessons in each situation and discover new options. Clarifies visions, imagery, astral travel and recall. Helps us replace fears and old ways with healthier ones. Cleans toxins and fumes from body. Needs cleansing if sticky. Fosters spirituality, creates peace, sweeping action to balance and clear the Chakras. Great for toxic fume damage. Used to eliminate infections and viruses. It provides a barrier to diminish the effect of disease-producing micro-organisms. Cleans out parasites. Called the money stone, green calcite brings back double any time you give. Used by Native Americans to enhance the annual Give-Away ceremony. Clears the body and the immediate environment of toxins.

Blue: Receptive. Element: Water. Eases pain (especially back pain). Uplifting, joy, happiness and humor. Fosters spirituality, creates peace, sweeping action to balance and clear the Chakras. Removes emotional blocks, balances one's emotional state. Reduces any feelings of intensity and overload. Often used during times of change and uncertainty. Increases the will and opens channels of communication.

Gold/yellow: Spine, bones. Detoxification of kidneys, pancreas, spleen. Decalcifying joints.

Clear/optical: Clearer vision and communication, wellness, general cleansing.

Orange: Projective. Element: Fire. Fosters spirituality, creates peace, sweeping action to balance and clear the Chakras. The higher wisdom and philosopher's stone. Creates a joyous attitude and sense of clarity. Spiritual evolvement is a result. Works with the third eye for intuition and to bring peace and protection to all the other Chakras. Banishes worry and anxiety. Used for headaches, tired eyes and releasing energy blocks. Also directs energy to specific points. Fosters spirituality, creates peace. Healing attributes: Works with improving the function of the kidneys, liver and spleen. Used to promote de-calcification of bone growths. Also aids in assimilation of calcium. It is called the happiness stone. Clears and creates an open mind while reducing skepticism. It is one of the most powerful protection stones, giving energy wherever held to the body. Orange calcite should be used with care as it is a powerful stimulant to the sacral Chakra. It is reported to restore lovers, heighten desire, increase sexual function and frequency. Calcite of orange attracts new love, enhances one's charisma and puts a smile on your face.

Chrysocolla (Gem Silica)

Receptive. Element: Water. Solid light blue/blue-green. Gentle, soothing, friendly. Excellent for heart chakra; flushes and heals heart blocks (loss, hurt, guilt, fear), flexibility, self-forgiveness, peace of heart, patience. Keeps one in light, love, and healing daily. On throat chakra; expressing feelings, verbal and artistic creativity, thyroid, heart, blood sugar, and emotional balance. High conductivity from Copper draws out pain, heat (fevers, inflammations, arthritis). Excellent therapeutic aid for healing loss, incest and other traumas. Cleanses auric field. Dreams and Earth healing. Supports letting go. Releases toxins physically and emotionally. Replaces anxiety with universal love. Drives off fear and illusion. Increases wisdom, attracts love. Major attractor of wealth and prosperity. Opens bottled emotions. Aids creativity. Hold in your left hand to dispel fears, illusions and negative thoughts. The colors of greenish/blue to almost white/blue are soothing and relaxing.

This is a stone that produces thoughts of peace and

restfulness. With worry banished, mental clarity is enhanced and problem-solving inspirations are unfolded. Recently Chrysocolla has been used to aid in ionizing the air. It purifies the environment either at home or at work. It processes negativity and assists in stabilizing a balanced atmosphere. It furthers understanding between people and releases animosity, guilt and frustration. An excellent tool for aiding communication blockages. It helps one remain silent when that is the best path. Or helps one to speak in their own behalf when such a course is desirable. Provides insight for healing. Chrysocolla works towards perfection in areas of bodily and emotional health. Has specifically been used in cases of asthma, TB, emphysema or any lung condition. It increases breathing capabilities. A number of users report visionary experiences when held to the third eye. A useful meditation tool and a practical enhancement stone for guided imagery.

Copper

Copper is perhaps one of the most useful magical metals in a magician's armory as it can be used with all forms of magick and spell casting. The magickal properties of Copper can be used for a whole multitude of things as it is one of the best energy conductors available and this certainly includes Magickal energies. Many magic wands are made of Copper for that very reason. In healing magick, Copper directs and focuses both electrical and physical energy, thus aiding in the body's healing processes. Copper amulets positively influence blood conditions and the body's circulation system, and Copper is said to protect the blood against disease due to its enhancing effects. These appear to include the stimulation of the blood's ability to carry and utilize oxygen, hormones and vitamins and to also enhance the blood's ability to carry away waste and toxic materials. Copper is also thought to enhance the body's immune system, strengthening its ability to ward off infections. It is popularly used as jewelry to ease many pains; that of sciatica, strained muscles and ligaments and used very widely in easing the discomfort of arthritis and rheumatism. Copper appears to have the property of greatly stimulating mental energies and therefore it enhances concentration and conscious awareness generally.

As it appears to have the property of revitalization and combating tiredness and lethargy, it is a handy force to have at hand. It is widely used to aid communication and channeling because of its ability to stimulate the mind and to conduct those psychic mental energies very well indeed. Copper is employed in cleansing and purification rituals, as it conducts negative energies away as easily as it conducts positive energies in. As well as healing magick, Copper's Magical properties mean it is used extensively in love magic, as it both attracts and strengthens emotional bonds. Being a magickal attractor, it is used in wealth and money spells as well as in general luck attracting. It is thought that Copper is associated with the deities Aphrodite and Ishtar. It is also associated with the deity Astarte.

Geodes

Receptive. Element: Water. Athletes and chess players, gamblers and entrepreneurs, job seekers and romance seekers... all love Oco geodes. Called the Victory Stone and related to the Goddess, Geodes are symbols of fertility and a companion to the creativity of the egg. Used worldwide to consecrate altars, ceremonies and new beginnings. They also are famous for bringing good luck and blessings. Use in weight management to easily see the desired self. One of the finer tools for self-empowerment. An unbelievable aid to visualization. Assists in understanding what one is viewing. Helps in traveling and in contacting spirit guides or totem animals.

A powerful shaman's stone. Here is the tunnel. The journey is waiting. A fantastic healer's and healing stone. Some pieces are convoluted on the outside and look much like the human brain.

Used for brain tumors. Excellent for balancing right brain and left brain activities. There is a combination of intuition and motivation for right action that leads to success. Raises self-esteem without creating ego.

Jade

Receptive. Element: Water. Solid to translucent green. Health, wealth, longevity stone. The ancient Chinese used jade for courage, wisdom, justice, mercy, emotional balance, stamina, love, fidelity, humility, generosity, peace and harmony. Jade is associated with the lungs, heart, thymus, immune, kidneys and blood detoxification, and the nervous system. Androgynous. A gentle, steady energy.

Nephrite

Sacred stone of protection. Integrates the subtle bodies of man into the subtle bodies of the Universe. Assists in balancing energies between partners, can also balance the male/female energies within each person. Used to stimulate white blood cells. Useful for recuperation from excess stress as it aids the adrenal glands. A recovery stone. Can regulate metabolism and often used for colic in children. In both Greece and Spain the name for the stone translates as 'kidney stone' for its aid to any complaints of the kidneys. Put some nephrite jade elixir in your bath water to help in releasing toxins. Especially helpful in cases of radiation poisoning. A calming and detachment stone from the emotional ups and downs of living. Great in dream work, both for analyzing and for working into lucid dreaming. Helps mental activity with clear judgment, increased ability for focus and concentration. Aids in promoting effortless self-discipline in any skill or endeavor. Builds self-esteem and confidence. Stimulates the adrenal glands, regulates metabolism and promotes white blood cells. Protection, wisdom and courage; forms a shield, boosts good luck and prosperity.

Kunzite

Receptive. Element: Earth. Spodumene with lithium. Pink, clear. Powerful, high level stone. Strengthens healers and teachers. Opens the emotional heart and the spiritual heart. Supports unconditional lovingness and compassion; healing from abuse/loss/addictions. Helps emotional balance, confidence, connection to higher self and oneness. Reduces depression, mood swings, stress, radiation. Brow and crown Chakras.

Deepens altered states, psychic readings, healing, being centered emotionally and spiritually.

Distinctive flattened crystals with deep striations. Encourages self-esteem and helps to remove insecurities. Relaxes your heart space. Enables pent-up thoughts and feelings to come out and be communicated in a thoughtful, caring manner. Simply dissolves negativity and fear. Works to contact spirit guides, angels, nature spirits and totem animals. Further enhances communication with these entities. Sets up a pathway for continuance of contact. Stimulates intuition while in meditation. Opens the doorway to the subconscious and provides a shield for unwanted energies. Used to eliminate energy blockages. Clears meridians and helps to reduce cholesterol. Works to strengthen the physical heart. Widely used for addictive disorders and calming nervous disorders. It is extensively mined for its Lithium content.

Obsidian

Projective. Element: Fire.
Solid/translucent black to smoky (including 'Navaho/Apache Tears'): Objectivity, disattachment, grounding. Protection, divination and peace. Reduces fantasy/escapism. Absorbs and dissolves anger, criticism, fear, etc. thus protective.

Black: Absorbs dark and converts to white light. Friendly. Can't be misused. Root Chakra. Brings higher Chakra light into lower ones; cleanses, uplifts. Changes fear into flexibility with change.

Snowflake: Clairaudience and owning our lower aspects for growth; healthy balance. (Be aware – obsidian balls help us to see truths by initially amplifying beliefs, patterns, fears, blocking our growth.) Spiritual powers: Brings purity and balance. Opens clarity for unwanted circumstances. Healing attributes: Used for creating smooth skin. Works with clearing veins and clearing eyes. Used to sharpen both the internal and external vision, one of the most important 'teachers' of the New Age stones, teaches one the truth of oneself in relation to one's ego, depicts the contrasts of life – day and night, darkness and light, truth and error. Serenity and relief.

Green: Heals broken crystals and charges them.

Prehnite

Spiritual powers: Dreaming and remembrance. Enhances one's protective field. Brings peace and calm. Healing attributes: Builds the immune system. Useful for anemia and other blood disorders. Clearly the color and unusual touch generate a serenity and tranquility uncommon even in the typical stress release stones. This is a most powerful stone. Has been used to aid in remembering dreams. Rub Prehnite just before going to sleep and ask for assistance in lucid dreaming. Due to its ability to rapidly move one into the other world, Prehnite has long been used as a secret stone of shamans. Because it can carry one into both the sub-conscious and the Earth's astral, it has become known as the 'Prediction Stone', and as such is much in demand by channelers.

Do not take Prehnite lightly. Before you go contacting entities make sure you have some understanding how to let them go, how to ascertain that you are truly in touch with the same energy (entity), and that you have some knowledge in limiting the vital life force any discarnate entity can absorb from you. Prehnite is par excellence for visualizations of any kind. It provides a smooth transition into meditation. One of the top stones available for self-hypnosis and auto-suggestion. In healing, Prehnite has been used to reduce high blood pressure and control hyper-tension. We have recently found that this remarkable stone can be used to balance meridians and also to activate (balance) acupuncture and acupressure points.

Quartz

Receptive/Projective. All elements. Clear, many forms and colors! Probably the most versatile multi-purpose healing stone. Easy to cleanse, store information and energy in, program or amplify energy and healing with energy. Can both draw and send energy. Powerful clear ones open brow, crown, and transpersonal Chakras for meditation, sending and receiving guidance. Stimulates natural crystals in body tissues and fluids to resonate at new healing frequency. Works with all Chakras and master gland.

All with Chlorite: Powerful for sending and advanced specialized uses.

Blue (or gray/lavender): A good healing stone for linking heart with throat and brow Chakras to expand self-expression and creativity, plus refining communication skills to new levels. Eases throat tension. Immune system, thyroid, iodine and B Vitamin use. Some say shining light through Blue Quartz can help reduce need for glasses. Still evolving. Yin.

Rose: Projective. Element: Fire. Translucent to clear pink. Love, beauty, peacefulness, forgiving, lovingness, self-love and emotional balance. Soft. Gently soothes and warms heart center. Emotional healing, loss, stress, hurt, fear, low confidence, resentment and anger. Slowly eases childhood traumas/neglect/ lack of love, low self-esteem. Cleanse and recharge often. Especially if fades. Aligns mental, emotional, and astral bodies. Spiritual: Self-acceptance, healing emotional wounds, stress, calm, peace and reducing haste. Healing: Clears body fluids, reduces wrinkles, clears skin, pain relief, coughs, burns, blistering and lungs.

Rutilated/Rutile: Clear Quartz with metallic, golden rutile, Copper, or blue/gray Titanium fibers that powerfully electrically conduct and amplify energy/thoughts/programming for healing. Intensifies/deepens altered states. Opens crown/brow Chakras for meditation, clairvoyance, telepathy and insight. Some make one too spacey or scattered to wear (induces Alpha states). Stimulates immunity, strength, blue corona, imagery and dreams. Golden fibers may increase radiation protection and health rejuvenation. Each stone's energy/qualities are unique. Androgynous.

Smoky Quartz: Two kinds: 1.) Smoky, root beer, or chocolate-colored clear crystals. The clearest, most intense ones powerfully open the crown Chakra drawing light down the root Chakra, inducing Alpha/deep meditation for channeling/higher guidance, deep relaxation, lovingness. Ancient use was also to stimulate the meridians, kundalini, and correct fertility/PMS/reproductive imbalance. Stores information well. Alleviates fear, anxiety, depression, emotional problems. 2a.) Dense, dull, solid/semi-solid black/brown, less attractive. Very grounding, opposite of other Smoky stones. May feel dense, heavy, non-conductive. 2b.) Many were irradiated to turn them this flat, dark color with white edge of base. If so, they're not useful for conducting light/healing, thus less useful for wearing or healing.

Tourmaline

A powerful, electromagnetic, striated gem. Strengthens body and spirit (and meridians), transmutes lower frequency thoughts/energy to a higher frequency of light and brings light/spirit into the physical. Radiates light protection for wearer. Clearer stones mean higher frequency and greater effectiveness, especially for the nervous system; blood/lymph toxins.

Black: Powerfully deflects/shields against unwanted or dark energies, especially for sensitive people. Grounds spiritual/light energy into the root chakra, for centeredness amid chaos. Neutralizes fears, resentment, neurosis, obsessions, intestinal or spine energy blocks, toxins, constipation. Place at feet, knees, or base of spine for grounding during/after healing. Radiation protection.

Blue (Indicolite): Wonderful for aligning with higher self for deep insight, vision, intuition, mental peace, patience, nerve system. Throat Chakra.

Green: Receptive. Element: Water. Taking heart, will to live, life force, prosperity, compassion. Energizes central nervous system (for neuralgia, migraine, burns, etc.). Opens/heals physical and emotional heart chakra (lungs, asthma, etc.). Cleanses meridians and blocks, stimulates new growth, rejuvenates heart, lymph and immune system. Thymus and entire body health. Yang.

Pink: Emotional and spiritual love, healing loss, emotional pain, fear, self-gentleness (especially with severe illness like cancer, emphysema, etc.). Best in combination with counseling. Most powerful together with Kunzite or Rhodocrosite. Self-love, compassion, release of old hurt. Trust.

Red: See Rubellite.

Watermelon: (Red/pink and green). Brings together compassion, passion, depth of heart with life force and grounding (red). Emotional and spiritual love (light pink) expressed in the physical heart Chakra (Green). Excels for immune system and life-threatening illnesses. Balances metabolism, endocrine system; harmonizing. Empowers other tourmalines. Yin/Yang balance.

Alexandrite

A Chrysoberyl. Clear violet-green, light blue or orange-yellow iridescence. Color changes with angle. Opens heart, solar plexus, and especially crown centers/Chakras. For healing, centering, self-esteem. Rare and powerful. Opens to higher self, disattachment, psychicness, spiritual love, joy, and luck. Excellent tissue regeneration; especially central nervous system.

Amber

Projective. Elements: Fire and Akasha. Clear yellow or orange ancient petrified resin (possibly pine tree). Electromagnetic. Opens solar plexus Chakra for mental clarity, mood balance and confidence. Stomach, anxiety, spine, central nervous system, brain, memory loss and cell regeneration. Excellent detoxification and protection from radiation, especially X-rays, sun, computers, airport, planes and others' energies. Sacred use (incense/worn) by Asian and American Indians, and worldwide. Energy magnet, increases enjoyment. Aligns mental and emotional bodies. High electrical charge for positive energy. Harmonizes Yin and Yang. Excellent in use in rituals for enhancing your beauty and attractiveness. Helps to attract love and stimulates happiness and pleasure. Used for both good luck and as a protective amulet and is extremely protective against negative magick which has been directed against you. Increased effectiveness of spells if placed on altar. Increases strength while relieving or curing health conditions. Protects children.

Amethyst

Receptive. Element: Water. Translucent, purple/lavender quartz. Psychicness, imagery and mind quieting. Wear when sleeping or when awake to reduce anger, impatience and nightmares. Brow and crown Chakras. Headaches, eyes, scalp/hair, pituitary, pineal and blood sugar balance. Especially aids sobriety; alcohol/food/sex/other addictions. Famous ancient detoxicifier (especially helps with poisons, alcohol.) Keep in pet's water to reduce fleas. Spiritual: Enhancing self-esteem, peaceful sleep, moderation, calmness, perception and opening one's spiritual side.

Healing: Headaches, assimilating foods, banishes pimples and rough skin, and treatment of arthritis. Enhances mind, intuition, insight and inner calm. Soul Stone. Eases compulsive/obsessive behavior (desire for food, tobacco, drugs, alcohol, etc.) calms an overactive mind, increases self-esteem, aids sleep. Spiritual, inner peace. Calms fears, reduces stress, dispels doubts and negativity, relieves depression and promotes good judgment. Includes vivid dreams, increases mental powers and is useful in psychicism. Draws pure, true, emotional love.

Aquamarine

A Beryl. Clear light blue, blue-green. Tranquilizing, uplifting, openness, innocence, light-heartedness, creativity, communication, self-awareness, confidence and purpose. Throat (and spleen) Chakras. Heart, immune system, thymus, lymph nodes, especially: mouth, ears, etc. Affects etheric and mental levels. Releases anxiety, fear, restlessness, peaceful stillness like the flow of a forest stream. Breathing allergies, water travel, journeys, sea goddess, seeing through people and protection.

Aragonite

Translucent purple-pink-brown hexagonal, or white needle crystals. Deep, peaceful meditation; uplifts emotions. Centering, overview, patience under stress, helps us navigate business/managerial/personal challenges with a clear head and steady hand. Giving and receiving easily. Balances Yin/Yang. Eyes, brain, central nervous system, heart, opens spiritual/brow Chakra for day-to-day living with an open heart and mind. Centering self during stress and anger. Problem-solving, patience and will power. Stimulates communication with higher plane.

Aventurine

Projective. Element: Air. Translucent dark/light green quartz. Heals emotional pain/fear/imbalance by dissolving blocks in the heart Chakra. Historically also draws out heat of fevers, inflammation, nervous system stress. Use in your bath water as a soft, soothing stone for general healing. Universal love, truth and prosperity. Much like Moss Agate.

Green: Spiritual: Protects the heart, enhances creativity, working with spirit guides, enables abundance and brings good luck and money. Healing: Works with lungs, heart, adrenal glands, calming troubled emotions and sexual organs. Joy, balance and clarity.

Peach: Spiritual powers: Personal power, draws prosperity. Used for contacting spirit guides. Inspires creativity. Healing attributes: Excellent for fertility, strengthening the urogenital systems.

Azurite/ Azurite-Malachite

Receptive. Element: Water. Solid deep blue, blue-purple. Activates brow and throat Chakras. more assertive communication and alert, quiet, deep access to subconscious and other times/places/lives. Psychicness, creativity, decisiveness, deeper insight, seeing truth, reduces depression, anger and abnormal cell growth. High Copper content stimulates thyroid, sinus, skin cleansing, spleen, nervous system, mental and etheric bodies.

Bloodstone

Projective. Element: Fire. (Heliotrope). Solid dark green, red flecks. Electromagnetic (high Iron). In Ancient Egypt and Atlantis it was used to calm, ground, revitalize. Classic stone for wealth, menstrual cramps, anemia, blood clots, hemorrhoids, birthing/ reproductivety and imbalance. Cleansing heart and blood circulation, marrow, thymus and lungs.

Boji Stones

Solid round, gray-brown discs with high Iron content. Grounding, electromagnetic. Balances the body's energy field. Many have found they reduce pain by holding a stone in each hand. Recharges electrically in sun. (Store Bojis apart – their magnetism neutralizes each other. Also, wearing or holding with a Tiger's Eye or other stone containing asbestos may bring on an ill feeling.)

Carnelian

Projective. Element: Fire. Chalcedony (Jasper) Quartz. Translucent. Confidence, boldness, initiative, dramatic abilities, assertiveness and outgoingness. Precision, analysis, appetite and awareness of feelings. Orange and yellow Chakras. Warms and cleanses blood, kidneys, stimulates appetite, emotions, passion, sexuality, physical energy, reproductive system, menstrual cramps, arthritis, kidneys, gall bladder and pancreas. Historically also used to pull excess fever out through the feet. Spiritual powers: Stone of courage. Helps to analyze. Banishes sorrow. Enhances will. Healing attributes: Improves skin disorders, used for allergies and colds. Works with PMS. Useful in spells relating to lust. Very helpful in all forms of healing. Can also be used to guard against people who try to read your thoughts.

Chrysoprase

Receptive. Element: Earth. Bright translucent green Chalcedony. Uplifts the heart Chakra. Greater flexibility, wisdom, generosity and self-confidence. Heals depression, excess self-focus and emotions/sexual imbalance. Placed on heart, neck, or on brow for meditation.

Citrine

Projective. Element: Fire. Clear yellow quartz. for solar plexus chakra, mental and emotional clarity. Problem-solving, memory, willpower, optimism, confidence, self-discipline and digestion. Reduces anxiety, fear, depression, stomach tension, food disorders and allergies. Detoxification: Spleen, kidneys, liver, urinary system, intestines, etc. Electromagnetic. Prevents night-mares and promotes a good night's sleep. Helps tap into user's power to give energy to magick. Can be used as a good luck stone. Increases self-esteem. Promotes creativity.

Coral

Receptive. Elements: Water and Akasha. Calcium and calcite.
Red and orange: stimulates 1st and 2nd Chakras for energy and warmth as well as fertility. Energizes emotions. Muscles, blood, heart, reproductive system; thyroid, metabolism; meridians; spine, bone and tissue regeneration. (Avoid if high blood pressure, fever, anxious.)

Pink: Heart Chakra, increases sensitivity, caring, compassion.

White: Soothes; heals meridians, stress, smell ability and nerves.

Black: Creativity, repels lower energies.

Danburite

Clear crystal. Powerfully radiates bright, pure, white light, filling the body, mind, and spirit (and relationships) with loving light. Excellent to cleanse, purify, or debrief. Fills third eye and crown Chakra with joy and illumination. Brings truth, honesty, a smile to the heart and opens receptivity to mind and spirit. Strengthens mind, nervous system, life force and awareness. Program for particular uses. Excellent healing tool.

Desert Rose

A Gypsum. Light brown. Gently grounding; clarifies thinking and mental vision, perception. Quiets worry, brings out practi-cality. (Related to Selenite). The spirit of these Selenite clusters send the message to stop, take time for self, smell the roses, find beauty in the day, and to enjoy every precious moment. You are reminded of the Divine in everything and everyone. The spirit here assists you in that joyous feeling of being connected.

Diamond

Projective. Element: Fire. (Carbon) Powerfully absorbs and amplifies thoughts/attitudes of user, other gems, and wearer's strengths and weaknesses. Prosperity, generosity vs. misery; love vs. distrust; overview, spirituality vs. lust, immediate gratification. Used with loving, clear intent; clears blocks, opens crown Chakra; spiritual love, peace. Clarity, trust and confidence. Cleanse thoroughly as it can hold others' previous attitudes and emotions. The ancients also used Diamonds for detoxification.

Dioptase

Tiny deep blue-green silicate crystals. Its powerful green reaches deep into the heart Chakra to release and heal sadness, heartache, abuse, neglect. Converts loss (recent/childhood) into self-love. Empowers heart with new depth, strength, healthiness, courage, ability to love deeply and unconditionally. Connects emotional heart with spiritual heart to receive abundance. Promotes genuineness, sincerity, emotional balance, self-worth and deep well-being. Central nervous system, lungs, heart, blood pressure and stress. Can send healing deep into the earth.

Dolomite

Pink/pastel/milky to clear. Clear varieties, especially pink, are used to softly open and heal the heart Chakra. Soothes hurt, loneliness, anxiety, etc. Facilitates giving and receiving, generosity, spontaneity, creativity and energy uplift. Calcium content strengthens bones, teeth, muscles, women's reproductive systems; helps PMS. Brings joy. Banishes sorrow. Calms and relaxes. Opens the heart. Works to reduce hyperactivity. Helps asthma, kidneys and adrenals. Radiates a soft energy of love that is hard not to notice. Aligns energy points. Can also be used to provide stoppage of any energy leaks. Encourages original and creative thinking. Type A personalities are benefited as well as hyperactive children.

Emerald

Receptive. Element: Earth. Beryl. Strengthens heart Chakra for abundance, growth, peace, harmony, patience, love, fidelity and honesty. Lifts depression and insomnia. Knowingness of the heart, peaceful dreams. Breathing, heart, lymph nodes, blood, thymus, pancreas (blood sugar rebalance), labor/delivery, eyesight, and etheric field. Excellent general healer. Ancient blood detoxifier and antipoison. Androgynous.

Epidote

Deep green, striated. Strengthens overall health, heart, well-being, energy. Courage, stamina. Helps take good care of one's self (food, rest, etc.). Ability to increase whatever one tunes into. It is the stone for all reasons. Augments personal power. Greatly enhances perception. Noted for its power in creating rapid spiritual awakening. Enhances intuition and perception. Powerful cleansing of emotional body. Use with caution. It releases pent-up emotions and opens blockages like no other stone.

Fluorite

Projective. All rainbow colors. Important balancer, healer. Opens heart (especially green), throat and two highest chakras for clarity, overview, seeing additional truths/realities. Spleen, bones, teeth, lungs, detoxification, anxiety, insomnia.

Clear and Purple: Objectivity; clears the way for new things, upliftment, aura cleanse, third eye, eyesight, sinuses; repels colds. Enhances other gems.

Green: Stills mind and heart, harmonizes and recharges all chakras.

Blue: Throat, nose, ears, soothing; karmic impasses resolved and atonement relieved.

Yellow: Focus, cooperation and group alignment.

Yttrium: Lavender, well-being, serenity, peace, connection with universe/God/eternal life force.

Clusters: Lowers work/life stress (helpful on your desk).

Double pyramid: Aligns spirit with physical plane, inner with outer awareness, and two sides/brain; crown chakra, illuminating karmic lessons. Spiritual: For spiritual growth, called the guidance stone, dissipates negativity, aids in concentration and memory. Healing: Canker sores, ulcers, heartburn, sore throat, infections and the intestinal tract. Opens wearer to influence of other stones. Grounds excess energy.

Garnet

Projective. Element: Fire. (Only clear Garnets are used for healing.)

Red: First and second chakras. Warms, energizes emotionally and physically (arthritis, frostbite, paralysis), grounds. Used by ancient cultures. Exhaustion, low BP, detoxing and strengthening blood, muscles, kidneys and gallstones. Stimulates life force and sexuality, hormone balance, antibodies, fertility, persistence, stamina, passion, confidence and stubbornness. Yang (avoid if suffering from excess anger, impatience, high blood pressure, heat, inflammation, etc.). First/root chakra.

Orange: Warmth, energy. Second chakra.

Gold

Excellent all-purpose, high-level gem amplifier and electrical conductor, especially on solar plexus and heart chakras. Strengthens meridians, nerve system, digestion. Positively charged with warming sun energy. Often worn by teachers/healers, especially after much self-healing (addictions, childhood). Attracts prosperity, stores and amplifies thoughts/emotions/energy (greed too). Yang.

Pink: Gold and Copper. Lovingness, warmth, spirituality.

White: Combines sun and moon energy, thus a higher conductor and amplifier.

Hematite and Marcasite

Projective. Element: Fire. Silver-gray metallic. (High Iron, Mercury). One of the most grounding of all stones (root chakra). Condenses scatteredness, fuzziness into mental clarity, concentration, memory, practicality, helps study, bookkeeping, detail work and sound sleep. Confidence, will power, boldness. The Egyptians used this stone to calm hysteria and anxiety. Yang. Helps us adjust to being physical. Associated with the spleen and blood, to cleanse. Can deflect. Regroups after jet lag, stress, birth and anesthesia. The mind stone, unlocks blockages, both cools and draws heat, banishes negativity, aids in concentration. Reinforces immune system, muscular aches and pains, blood disorders, leg cramps and fractures. Grounding and centering, focus and self-discipline. Good for scrying. Draws illness out of the body.

Jasper

Chalcedony Quartz, multi-colored, solid. Yellow, orange, brown, green.

Green: Receptive. Element: Earth. Respiratory/heart chakra. General tissue regeneration; mineral assimilation; general healing.

Darker colors: more grounding. (Also less conductive for healing.)

Red: Projective. Element: Fire. Spiritual: Most powerful energy stone, stimulates sexual energy, protection, pacing and Shamanic journeying. Healing: For liver, kidneys, bladder, aura cleansing and for extended hospitalization when energy is low.

Yellow: Spiritual powers: Aids memory retention. Activates will. Heightens awareness. Brings clarity. Healing attributes: Regulates the nervous system. Soothes the digestive and urinary tracts. Yellow for stomach, intestines, liver, spleen areas, earthy grounding.

Lapis Lazuli

Receptive. Element: Water. Solid, medium to dark blue. In meditation, opens brow chakra; higher guidance, intuition, connection to higher self, overview, decisions for good of all. Organizes, quiets mind. Opens throat/thyroid chakra; self-expression, writing, creativity, dream insight. Anxiety, restlessness, insomnia, autism, shyness, nervous system; MS, speech, hearing, pituitary, DNA, lymph, inflammation, pain (especially head) and protection.

Lodestone

Metallic black, natural magnet. Related to (and works like) Hematite for grounding, clear thinking, focus (detail work, decisions, etc.). Electromagnetically pulls toxic blocks and pain from energy meridians, pancreas, and lower glands. There is an old story of its use for a faithfulness test – the unfaithful one is said to fall out of bed if touched by this stone.

Malachite

Receptive. Element: Earth. Steady pulsing electromagnetic energy. (High Copper content). On brow: Stimulates physical and psychic vision, concentration. For heart and solar plexus centers: Stomach, liver, kidney stones, lungs, immune system, radiation, MS, circulation. Powerful with Azurite or Chrysocolla for healing. Releases and draws out pain, inflammation, depression, anger; heals blocks. Protects well by powerfully cleaning the auric field, rapidly absorbing undesirable energies, including: computer, TV, and other radiation, etc. Place in the four corners of a room to cleanse carpet toxins/gases. Clean very frequently – daily if possible! Increases power to send power toward your magickal goal. Used in protective magick. Travelers' guardian stone. Relaxes the nervous system and calms stormy emotions. Promotes tranquility and ensures sleep if worn to bed. Held, it dispels depression.

Moldavite

Greenish to brown-green Tektite (fell to Earth). Dull outside, deep clear green inside. Powerfully expands psychicness, channeling. On heart chakra, eases longing to leave earth. On pillow, brow, crown: Telepathic access to spiritual laws, info from higher regions/places to help us and Earth to be healthier and more spiritual. An intense meteorite helping people incarnating from elsewhere be more comfortable here on Earth (reducing asthma, toxin sensitivity, emotional intensity and epilepsy). May make some too spacey; be sure to ground self after use and before driving. Fragile – don't salt cleanse! More rare, expensive and powerful than a plain 'tektite'.

Moonstone

Receptive. Element: Water. Feldspar (contains Aluminum). Translucent with white, pink, yellow, soft sheen. Soothes stress, anxiety, women's hormones/menstrual imbalance and lymph. Enhances intuitive sensitivity via feelings and less overwhelmed by personal feelings. Greater flexibility and flow with life. Connects second and sixth chakras and pineal for emotional balance and gracefulness. Helps all be more comfortable with our gentler feminine/Yin receiving side. Especially useful for those born under astrological water signs.

Onyx

Projective. Element: Fire. Protective. Balances and grounds. Absorbs and flattens emotional intensity. Androgynous. Can't conduct or retain healing energy/programming very well.

Black: Root chakra. Grounding. Protection, defensive magick. Great for defense against negativity. Can be used to reduce sexual desires. Onyx is an extremely potent protective stone and is widely known for its ability to protect against psychic attacks and hexes.

Green: Heart/fourth chakra.

Yellow: Third chakra, seriousness, logic.

Blue: Fifth chakra. The more translucent/clearer ones are more effective.

Opal

Receptive/projective. All elements. A silicate. Contains water, correlating with our emotions. Clarifies by amplifying and mirroring feelings, buried emotions, desires (including love and passion). Less inhibition, more spontaneity. Crown and brow chakras. Visualization, imagination, dreams and healing. Easily absorbs, stores emotions and thoughts. Fragile. Fades/cracks in sun, heat, salt, acidic foods. Moisten frequently with water or oil. Some cancel/negate other gems (backfires if not used for good of all). May change color with high energy/intensity people.

White: Balances left/right brain.

Black/dark blue: One of the most potent.

Fire Opals: May stimulate passion, temper, energy.

Pearl

Receptive. Elements: Water and Akasha.

White: Symbol of pure heart and mind; innocence, faith. Of the sea, it has watery and lunar elements, thus balancing emotions, especially for water signs. Absorbs thoughts, emotions. For solar plexus chakra (digestion, stomach, immunity) and emotional stress. Low integrity or anger rebounds to user (like Opal). Cleanse frequently. Fire signs less compatible unless drawn to Pearl. May cool and soothe.

Gold and black: Also for prosperity.

Pink: Works especially with the heart chakra. Pearls work best without other gems. Divers wear for shark protection.

Petrified Wood

Receptive. Element: Akasha. Spiritual: For grounding, seeing into past lives, getting rid of worries, and stabilizing. Healing:

Strengthening bones and skeletal system, backache, and to stimulate thickness and luster in hair.

Pyrite (Fool's Gold)

(With Iron). One of the most grounding stones in use today. Used for focus, practicality, logic, memory, clearing fuzzy thinking/scatteredness, etc. like Hematite. Helps yellow Chakra: Stomach, intestines, ulcers; sulfur and mineral assimilation, circulation, body acidity imbalances, depression, illusions/lack of clarity about situations/people. Great for grounding spaciness after meditation/psychic readings. Represents the sun's golden energy.

Ruby

Projective. Element: Fire. Red corundum. Contains chromium (blood sugar balance). Warms, energizes after exhaustion. Strengthens physical and emotional heart (fourth chakra), love, courage, confidence, vitality, stamina, strength, leadership and success over challenges. Intensifies all emotions (passion, jealousy, impatience, love). Attempted use for pressure/control (for love, etc.) backfires onto user. Used for reproductive/root chakra; infections, cholesterol, clots, blood detox (alcohol, caffeine, etc.), sexual blocks. Stimulates circulation, menses, pituitary and healing the Earth.

Sapphire

Receptive. Element: Water. Corundum. Blue, green, pink, purple, clear. Related to Ruby.

Blue: Communication, insight, intuition, clairaudience, inspiration, spiritual prayer/devotion, peacefulness. Detoxing skin, body. Antidepressant. Cools, contracts, soothes, thus reducing inflammation, fevers, nosebleeds. Hearing problems, TB, burns, etc. Nervous system (and epilepsy) and meridians. Strongest if next to skin, especially the throat chakra.

Star: Wisdom, will, centering, cheerfulness, luck. Reduces radiation effects, anxiety, procrastination. Some effects subtle. Black: More grounding. Protection. May strengthen by posing challenges to overcome.

Selenite

Element: Water. A Gypsum. White/clear striated crystals. Mental focus, growth, luck, immunity, kundalini. Centuries-old record keepers of events/information. Smoothes emotions. Holding crystal, visualize it bringing white light/energy (higher ideas/consciousness) from transpersonal point above head down through body, out through feet into earth/physical plane. Place on the third eye for stored info. May help physical and emotional letting go. Reproduction, spine and nervous system, emotional and athletic flexibility. Sends healing to the earth. Expands sensitivity, field of awareness.

Serpentine

Projective. Element: Fire. Protection, lactation. Guard against poisonous creatures. Spiritual powers: Assists visualization and meditation. Aids in raising the Kundalini. Clears chakras. Healing attributes: Eliminates parasites, helps diabetes and hypoglycemia. Best used when directing the energies.

Staurolite (Fairy Cross)

Elements: Earth, Air, Fire and Water. Brown/grey, cross-like extrusions. Represents the four elements and joining of spirit with earth/matter. Spirituality, compassion, allowingness, disattachment. Focus centered on the here and now.

Sulphur

Projective. Element: Fire. Solid/clear yellow. Rejuvinating, especially if one does a great deal of thinking/mental work and little physical exercise. Mental clarity, focus, analysis, understanding, willpower, discipline, confidence. Used in Egypt and modern hot springs/baths for arthritis, pain, rheumatism, swelling, lymph, cysts and hemorrhoids. Traditionally very healing for wounds, cleansing and healing skin, sinus, pancreas, liver, syphilis, appendix, indigestion, insomnia, depression, etc. Strengthens endocrine glands. Found in garlic, mustard, chives, onions, horseradish, etc. Repels garden bugs. Third chakra. Helps to eliminate negative thoughts and emotions. Good for flashes of inspiration and as aid to self-growth and perfection. Used in protective rituals or in home as a general magickal ward.

Sunstone

Projective. Element: Fire. Aventurine feldspar with gold-orange metallic sheen. Warms the heart and lifts/rejuvinates the spirit. Protection, life force, grounding. Energy, health and sexual energy.

Tanzanite

Clear, blue-purple-violate Zoisite crystal. (Use clear ones for healing meditation.) Placed on brow, it powerfully opens brow plus crown centers for clairaudience, visions, spiritual connectedness, protection, manifesting. Helps expand our physical and mental seeing, hearing, hair, skin.

Thulite

Avocado green with patches of pinkish red. Balances the four lower chakras. These are often thought the most difficult to bring into line as they affect our desires, sensuality, will and emotions. A marathon runner's stone. Works with breathing and allocation of energy. A creator's dream as focusing on Thulite brings one quickly into altered states of consciousness with the ability to perceive inspiration when presented. Aids in answering questions involving love and logic. A healer's dream too, as this stone can be worn or taped to the body for rapid absorption of its healing energies. Works well with the intestine, lower bowel and helps with pre-menstrual problems. Has been used successfully for fertility. There is a toxin release and an immune building combination that makes this a fine candidate for any weight management program.

Tiger

Projective. Element: Fire. Chalcedony Quartz Cat's Eye. Yellow-gold. Confidence, willpower, clear thinking (and thus speaking), personal power in life. Yellow/solar plexus chakra. (Not as strong as citrine or Topaz.) Works on mental plane; amplifies thinking and manifesting what you think about (careful!), will. Helps separate thoughts from feelings, so centered, less emotional. Digestion, stomach, anxiety, ulcers and bones. Use with Malachite or Pearl for mental/emotional balance, understanding. Helps change anxiety, fear and obsessiveness into practicality, logic, etc. Yang.

Green or Blue: See Hawk's Eye (in other publications, not listed in this book).

Topaz

Golden or pink/'Champagne' crystal.

Golden: The most powerful, electromagnetic of yellow/solar plexus gems. A strong, steady, high-level gem for mental clarity, focus, perceptivity, high level concepts, confidence, personal power and stamina. Helps mood swings, insomnia, worries, fears, depression, exhaustion, nervous system stress and stomach anxiety. Also works somewhat with the crown chakra. Liver/pancreas detoxification, blood sugar balance, tissue and backbone strengthener (physically and emotionally). Radiates warmth, sun/light energy and protection. Excellent for water signs, teachers, excess work stress, manifesting, higher-self connection. Brings emotions and thinking into balance.

Pink and Champagne: Works also especially with the heart

for love, spiritual compassion.

Blue: Alignment with our higher self, creative expression, writing, focus on your path.

Turquoise

Receptive. Element: Earth. Light blue/blue-green. A good general healer for all illnesses and excellent conductor (high Copper). This gentle, cool, soothing stone is a Native American classic. It opens the throat chakra for open communication, creativity, serenity, spiritual bonding, upliftment. Opens the heart chakra for giving/receiving. Symbolizes our source (spirit/sky) and spiritual love for healing, help. On brow: Psychic connection to Great Spirit. Strengthens and aligns all meridians, chakras, and energy fields. Like Amethyst, it protects and detoxes from alcohol, poison, pollution, X-ray/sun radiation. Ancient absorber of 'negativity'; protection from 'evil eye'. Brings wisdom. Helps anorexia, headache, fear, etc. Throat, lungs, asthma, infections, teeth, TMJ, hearing, high blood pressure, creativity block and depression.

Dull, paler means weaker. Works well with Chrysocolla, best with Silver. Used for healing on every continent! Androgynous, balances Yin/Yang. Fades in sunlight, sweat, oil, dishwater. Avoid bleach/chlorine!

Zircon

All colors. Clear, colorless, natural form: Works with the crown chakra and transpersonal point (and pituitary and pineal) for Universal Truth, intuition, durability, steadiness, integrity and connection with 'All That Is.' Eases depression and insomnia. Also historical poison detoxifier. Man-made (Cubic Zirconia or 'CZ') is not nearly as strong/effective as natural. 'Pink Ice' is pink CZ.

Crystals Not Suitable For Water Cleansing

Selenite is severely damaged by water, it can dissolve if left in water and even a little contact with water will damage it. Angelite and Celestite also dissolve in water.

Malachite is toxic and should not be used with water at all.

Sulphur, also toxic, should not be used with water, wash hands after handling this.

Raw Kyanite: OK to water cleanse tumbled Kyanite, raw Kyanite will become damaged in water.

Jet has been known to get damaged by water.

Azurite is damaged by water.

Other methods of cleansing are: Earth cleansing; burying the crystal in your garden for a few days. Sun cleansing; leaving your crystals in the sunlight for a few hours, some stones are better cleansed in the sun, Carnelian, Sunstone, Citrine, Quartz and Jasper to name a few. Moon cleansing; leaving your crystals in the moonlight overnight. This is especially beneficial for Moonstone, blue light Goldstone, rainbow Moonstone, Nebula stone and Nuumite to name some. Inner light cleansing; meditation bathing your crystals in a cleansing light. Can be used for any crystal. Smudging; using smoke from slow burning herbs (usually sage) or incense to cleanse your crystals.

Magickal Properties of Wood

All forms of natural wood contain within them energies derived from the Earth. These energies, if used properly, can greatly increase the Magick, Rituals and healing work that you choose to participate in. Once again, only a small listing will be provided here. Those woods listed in this section will be of substantial importance!

Alder

Alder is considered to be the 'witches' wood. It has many magickal and non-magickal powers. This tree can be used to make three different colored dyes, red, from the bark (which symbolizes fire), green from the leaves (symbolizing water) and brown from the twigs (symbolizing earth).

A whistle may be made from its wood that can summon the four winds and it is also used to create flutes and magickal pipes. Because of this, it has been used to control or banish Elementals.

Alder is associated with the God Bran as it indicates protection and oracular powers.

Ash

The branches of the Ash are used in making wands and in protection spells. It has long been believed that special guardian spirits are contained within the wood of this tree, which make it especially useful for absorbing and dispelling sickness.

Sacred to Poseidon and Woden, it is considered the tree of the resident power found in water.

Ash is especially useful for spells requiring focus or strength and indicates the linking of the outer and inner worlds. It is also well serviced in areas of karmic law, healing and protection.

Birch

Birch is associated with fertility and agriculture. Among its many uses are cleansing rituals and healing. It is used to drive away evil spirits and rods of Birch were used to drive off the spirits of the old year.

It has been historically used as the primary wood used for making children's cradles due to its nature. It was a common practice to give newlyweds Birch twigs to increase fertility. Birch twigs were also used for fertility for cattle and fields, to ensure an abundance of food.

Birch is influenced by its lunar nature and is associated with the Goddess.

Cedar

This tree and its wood are often used to create and maintain sacred spaces. Placed above a door, it will repel negative energies and influences. The shavings and powdered wood are burnt to dedicate a sacred space. In the Native American belief (Cherokee), it is believed to hold powerful ancestor spirits since the beginning of existence.

Cedar is used in solar spells to strengthen and illuminate your focus.

Oak

The mighty Oak is the tree of triumph and endurance. A masculine wood, it is used to create Athames, specific rods and Wands. The Midsummer fire should always be of Oak wood because it imbues stamina, strength, power and prosperity.

This wood is also considered a guardian and liberator.

Rowan

This tree has long been seen as the tree of life. It has long been viewed as a protection from enchantment. Each berry carries a small pentagram on its surface, lending to its protective quality.

The ancient Celts used Rowan wood to carve into runes for divination.

It is used in Astral work, protection, divination and healing.

Willow

Sacred to Hecate, Circe, Hera and Persephone; it is associated with the moon and the Crone aspect of the Triple Goddess. It is a symbol of mourning, but its wood can be used to create tools to make wishes come true.

It indicates the cycles, ebb and flow. Because of this it is often used in love, healing and fertility rites.

Yew

This tree has long been associated with death. Rebirth, magick and the Runes.

It may be the oldest existing tree and is known as the death tree across Europe.

Yew can be used to enhance Magickal or psychic abilities; but should not be used for any Magickal tools!

Phase Three

Internal and External Power
(Self-Discovery and Using Energy)

The more man meditates upon good thoughts; the better will be his world and the world at large.
Confucius

During your travels through the first two phases of your training, you have been shown that energy; power and Magick can be found in all of the things the Goddess has provided for us, even the earth beneath our feet. The power to create and heal is already there, the energy to follow through on these things has been provided as well.

Before you can use these things appropriately and well, you must first learn to harness the energies within so that you may use the energy that is all around you. As a member of the Clergy, you must understand how to channel in to your Higher Self easily and direct the flow of energies for creation and healing.

To control and focus these energies requires an understanding of what is within you (and every other being on this planet) and be able to use it in a constructive manner.

In the following lessons, we will begin to learn how to achieve these things. Learning how to use the tools will serve you no purpose in the later lessons unless you practice; practicing with those tools and becoming proficient with them is the only way these tools will be of any use at all.

Meditation (Entering Your Higher Self)

Meditation is a practice dating back many thousands of years. It is a tool used for clearing the mind, developing focus, healing, self-evaluation and attaining the Higher Self (that part of you which is unencumbered by the social pressures and anxieties of this world).

There are many forms of meditation and each has value. Our goal here is to help you attain a state of consciousness that will allow you a more clear and personal contact with Deity.

You have already used a simple form of meditation in the grounding and centering exercises. When preparing for Ritual, you might consider a more complete grounding. This entails much of what you have already learned, but with some minor additions.

Using the techniques you learned earlier, ground and center yourself. Now, instead of allowing yourself to immediately return, remain a moment and visualize a sanctuary. Look around what you have created. Find a focal point. I use a pool of water that reflects everything around it. From this point visualize a radiance rising from it; you should begin experiencing a sense of calm and peace. Allow this radiance to float to you and merge with your spirit, this is your Higher Self. Once you feel completely joined with it, slowly begin to return to the place and time you were in at the start of the process, but do not let go of the essence that has joined you (you will release this essence at the end of Ritual). In this state, you will be more in tune with Deity and all of the surrounding energies, allowing you to be a much more effective instrument for the task at hand.

Many techniques for meditation are available. Here is but one method (as you progress, as with everything you are learning, you will eventually develop a method that is best suited to you):

Take three deep breaths, letting yourself relax. Imagine your consciousness drifting down into the Earth, as you keep breathing slowly and deeply, and then your consciousness comes to rest somewhere inside the Earth, where you find a place with a certain mineral in it that you feel attracted to. See this mineral start to glow, becoming brighter with colored light, whatever color you like.

Now see the light become a beam, and it is moving up now, all the way up until it enters the bottom of your right foot. Then become aware of your right foot, how it feels, and see the light begin to move up your right leg, and become aware of your right leg. Then, see the light continue to go up your right side, as you become aware of that area, then it enters your right hand, and continues up your right arm to the shoulder. Become fully aware of your whole right side, and see the light illuminating the whole right side of your body. Now move the light cord over to your left shoulder, and become aware of that area. Now the light begins moving down your left arm, hand, fingers, and you feel it moving down your left side, as you focus your awareness to your left side. Then the light cord moves down your left leg, into your left foot. Become fully aware of all sensations in the whole left side of your body. The light finally continues back down into the Earth, where it connects back to its source, completing the circuit. The light is continually in motion, moving up from the Earth up your right side as you breathe in, and circulating back down your left side and back to its source as you breathe out. Feel this energy revitalizing you as you breathe and relax.

Now see a third energy cord come up out of the Earth, perhaps of another color, and it enters your body at the base of your spine, the first Chakra. See that Chakra as a wheel of light, which fills up with this new energy and begins to glow brightly, and starts to spin. As it does this, any negative energies, fears, or blockages begin to clear out, and you see it spinning in perfect alignment with your spine as an axle. See the top of the first Chakra open up, and see the energy beam move up into the second Chakra. Continue moving the beam up into each successive Chakra, seeing each one clear out and start to spin, all the way up to the seventh Chakra at the crown of your head. Then see the energy beam shoot up out of the top of your head, showering your whole body with light, which surrounds and protects you from any unwanted energies.

The Casting of the Circle

Casting the Circle is one of the most important things a practitioner of the Craft will learn. Once cast, the Circle will be used for any number of things, healing, protection, amplifying energy for projection; the list goes on and on. As a member of the Clergy, you will use it for all of these things, but it is the primary tool in preparation for any and all Ritual. You are now going to learn the correct process for casting. The methods you may use may change over time, but the order in which they are done must never change.

First, you must determine where your sacred space is to be created. If this is for a personal and private objective, you need only enough area to encompass yourself and the tools you will be using. If the Circle is to be used for a public Ritual, the area must be large enough to surround all those in attendance. It is very important that all who attend must be surrounded by the protective energy of the Circle so that there is no chance of negative energies entering due to the movement of the attendees. As a matter of course, you should recognize the fact that people will move around. If your Circle is not large enough, that movement may cause an individual to accidentally step out of the Circle, in effect breaking the protective barrier and opening your Circle to negative energy. This can do great harm to the intent of the ritual. Preparing in advance is the best way to avoid this issue.

When preparing to cast the Circle, it is wise to use the techniques you learned on attaining the Higher Self. This will provide a greater aspect of energy control and make the process much more effective.

Now is when you decide the placement of your Altar (if it is portable). Should you be in a position where you have a permanent Altar you have already made this choice. Generally, as discussed in the First Phase, the Altar is placed in the Northern area of your Circle. If your Ritual is to be held outside, it would be wise to make the outer edges of it visible for your attendees (once again, to keep them from accidentally straying out and breaking the Circle). Once this is done, it is time to go about the business of preparing the space.

You need to cleanse the space of negativity. If you are using a portable Altar, you should first cleanse the place the Altar will be and then arrange your Altar. You may use any of the cleansing techniques that were discussed in Phase One for this purpose. After the Altar is placed, continue cleansing the space until every part has been covered. Depending on the number of attendees, this could be somewhat time-consuming. Plan accordingly so that your space is ready at the appointed time ('Pagan Central Time' is not an appropriate tool).

Now you can create (cast) the Circle. If this is to be a public ritual, you may wish to allow the attendees to witness this event. It can set them in a receptive mood and make your Ritual much stronger. Make sure that anyone who is not actually participating in the casting is outside the boundary line. The guests will enter only at the time and place you have decided upon.

I am providing here details of a casting that I have used for a number of years. Once again, as you progress you will use others, create your own and become comfortable with them. This is merely an example:

Gather everything for your Ritual, Make sure you will not have to leave your circle and break it. I use an altar, and place it in the North, representing manifestation. Next you'll need something to represent the Earth Element, a rock or salt. Place it in the North of your pentacle (Circle). Next, you'll need something to represent East, the Air Element. You can use incense or feathers. Place that in the East of your Circle. Next, you'll need something that represents South, the Fire Element. A candle or maybe a lava rock would do. Place it to the South of your Circle. Next, you'll need something that represents West, the Water Element. You can use a chalice, a bowl of water, or a seashell. Place it to the West.

After you have done this and have everything for your Ritual, you may close your Circle with the chalk or string. Sit inside your Circle when you're ready to cast a spell and outline your Circle with your wand and say: 'I cast this Circle to protect those herein from outside influences; I charge this Circle to bring in only loving and helping vibrations. I create a sacred space.'

Outline your Circle again saying: 'I cast this Circle to bring in positive magick only, all negativity leave my Circle now. I create this sacred space.'

Next, stand in your Circle with your wand, athame or sword. Point your wand to the North and say: 'Oh great and beautiful Gods, Goddesses, and Guardians of the North – Power of Earth – I call you to attend my circle.'

Turn and point your wand to the East and say: 'Oh great and beautiful Gods, Goddesses, and Guardians of the East – Power of Air – I call you to attend my circle.'

Turn to the South and point your wand and say: 'Oh great and beautiful Gods, Goddesses, and Guardians of the South – Power of Fire – I call you to attend my Circle.'

Turn to the West and point your wand and say: 'Oh great and beautiful Gods, Goddesses, and Guardians of the West – Power of Water – I call you to attend my Circle.'

You may now announce: 'The Circle is whole, enter in love and peace.'

The Circle is now cast. Move to the place that you wish your attendees to enter (the entry will be small so it is suggested that they enter single file), with your athame, cut an arch counterclockwise from the ground up and back to the ground. This creates an entrance for your guests without compromising the Circle.

A practice many include in their Rituals is when the attendees enter, to have one or two acolytes asperge (using the blessed salt and water and a feather) the people entering the Circle to dissipate any negative energy clinging to them. During the processional entrance, the High Priest may at the direction of Deity challenge anyone entering the sacred space. This is not an arbitrary act. All negative energies must be kept out of the space for it to hold and be effective. We will cover what causes a challenge and how it is done later in your training.

Once the guests are all inside the Circle, the High Priest will close the entrance he created by reversing the action that was used to open it. Once closed, *no one* may leave the Circle without a doorway first being prepared. Anyone leaving without a doorway will cause the Circle to dissipate and damage the Ritual. All those planning to be inside the sacred space need to be made aware of this prior to entering!

Releasing (Closing) the Circle

Once the ritual is complete, the Circle may be released or closed. This may be done while the guests are still inside the space or after they have left. If you choose to wait until they are outside the space, you need to open an exit (just as you created the entrance) and close it again once all are outside. Releasing the Circle is as important as the casting because it releases the power and energy used to Deity and serves to increase and charge the work done within the Circle.

This example is one of the simplest methods of releasing the Circle. Though not as elaborate as most, it is still an acceptable method:

When you have completed your rites, you must release the Circle.

Hold your wand up while facing North and say: 'Farewell. Spirit of the North, I give thanks for your presence here. Go in power.'

Repeat this to the East, South, and West (substituting the correct direction in the ritual). Lay the wand on the altar and pick up the Athame, Stand at the north edge of the circle and place the blade at the wall of the circle, holding it at waist level. Move clockwise around the Circle visualizing the power of the Circle being sucked back into the blade once you arrive at the North again.

Say: 'The Circle be closed but unbroken, go in peace.'

The circle is now released.

Energy Raising

Energy raising; this is a tool that you will forever be learning and relearning, refining your techniques over time to become much more effective in all aspects of your Clerical Path.

You have already learned how to start. By aligning your conscious mind with the Higher Self, you become more open to the energies found all around you. These outside energies are found in every single thing that is around you. The effect of raising these energies and drawing them to you is an amazing feeling. When you have achieved this, it can be very exciting. It is much like the sensation of static electricity on the body and even the mind. Once you learn to harness and focus these things, you will be shocked by what you can do. At this point, we are not concerned with direct focus; but rather a general focus. The energies you raise here are useful only in strengthening the conduit between your intent and Deity in an effort to concentrate that intent.

In the beginning, while you are refining your techniques, you may have to actively use visualization to achieve your goal. As you progress, you will find it less important as you will begin to see these energies around you. This takes time and the ability to truly align your physical being with your Higher Self. The only means of creating this alignment is through consistent practice. True alignment places you in a state much more in contact with Deity and because of that you can see and feel many things that essentially cannot be reached on the physical plane.

Start by using the techniques for entering your Higher Self. Focus on the intent of why you are asking for this elevated energy. It cannot be stressed enough that your **intent be of a positive nature**, anything else will lead to failure and could drain energy from you in the process. Once you have achieved that state, let your mind look around you. See all the things as they are on the physical plane at first. As you continue to look around, allow your third eye and crown chakras to become active (in the Higher Self, this will occur naturally). Now see deeper into the plane you are truly on. As your Higher Self draws you onto that plane, you will begin to see shimmering (faint at first). Visualize these shimmers as balls of energy as discussed in the section Grounding and Centering. Make this energy become denser, taking on a solid aspect. As this energy reaches its most solid point, focus on drawing some, but not all, of that energy into yourself. As that power enters you, allow Deity to control how much. She will help with how much energy is needed for your intended purpose. It is always best to start small. **Do not enter this in the beginning with the idea that you are going to Magickally change things, you are not ready.** Expect only those things that will enhance your Ritual at present. Without training and knowledge, you can do great harm; both to others and yourself. Keep ever present in your mind the 'Harm None' tenet of the Rede that we follow.

Every living being has the internal ability to achieve these things; it is due to both social and religious pressure over the centuries that we have lost the capacity to use them. Given the key, having the desire and working with it will allow you to open those doors in your subconscious and once again be able to use the tools the Goddess has provided us.

Cleansing Water for Ritual

Many will have on hand water that has been blessed and charged for the Ritual cleansing of a sacred space, for the removal of negative energies, etc. Although it far pre-dates the Christian version (theirs is based on the practice of the Old Ways), it is basically a form of holy water. This water can be used for a number of things; protection, removing negative energy, even exorcising unwanted negative spirits (once you are familiar with the techniques).

The amounts included can be modified to make a larger quantity, just make sure the ratios remain the same. This was written to cleanse a single Circle.

Formula for 'Holy Water'
1 tsp. of rose water (optional)
3 tbs. sea salt
1 small bowl of spring water
1 clean glass container
1 new compact mirror
1 storage bottle (small)

Before the ritual, cleanse and sterilize the bowl and glass container with boiling water. Ensure that you have total privacy during preparation.

Ritual time: Midnight during a full moon phase.
Ritual place: Out of doors under the moon, or near a window that will reflect the light of the moon.

Set out your work cloth and all ingredients upon it. Take five or six deep breaths to relieve the stress of the day. Cast your magick Circle. Hold your arms outstretched in the Goddess position (arms out at the sides like you are cradling the Universe, palms up).

Say: 'In the cloak of the midnight hour I call upon the Ancient Power I seek the presence of the Lady and Lord to bless this water that I will pour.'

At this point, you should feel the energy of Earth Mother and Sky Father move about your feet and head. Feel your own energy expand around your navel and then unite with Divinity. Take your time; no need to rush. Add the rose water to the spring water. Pick up the bowl of water, hold it toward the light of the moon.

Say: 'In my hands I hold the essence of the Gods. I hereby cleanse and consecrate this water to Divinity that it may be used for positive acts only and may aid me in my magickal work.'

Feel the energy of the Moon Goddess pulsate down into the water. Imagine her silver light descending from the heavens and impregnating both the water and yourself. You will feel a 'glowing' sensation. Set the water down and pick up the salt. Feel the power moving in your arms as you raise the salt toward the moon.

Say: 'In my hands I hold the essence of Earth Mother, She whose bounty sustains all living creatures. I hereby consecrate this salt to Divinity that it may be used for positive acts only and may aid me in my magickal work.'

As with the water, imagine the energy of the Moon Goddess empowering the salt. Set the salt down and pour a little into the bowl of water, and stir clockwise three times. Repeat this process twice more. With the bowl in your left hand (receiving) and the mirror in your right (sending), reflect the light of the moon off the mirror and into the bowl.

After a few moments, say: 'This liquid is now pure and dedicated to the Lord and Lady. It is free from all negativity in any time and any space.'

Phase Four

Reaching the Crest (Using it Wisely)

How we think shows through in how we act. Attitudes are mirrors of the mind. They reflect thinking.
David Joseph Schwartz

As you proceed in both your Path and your day-to-day life, you will see advertisements selling magic spells... love spells, revenge spells and so many other things like this. Before you proceed, look back at the many things you have learned so far. Now, ask yourself, do these things you see for sale by so many 'Pagan' suppliers seem to fit the Path? Do they fulfill the Rede as we have learned?

In your answer, you should see the reason for this phase of learning. Take this phase to heart and hold it closely, what you learn here will be in all likelihood the most important subject matter you will be provided on your Clerical Path. It will affect your actions throughout the remainder of your life on the Path.

The Ethics of Wytchcraft

Ethics is defined as:

eth·ics [éthiks] *n npl*
[15th century. Via Old French *ethiques* < Greek *ēthika* < *ēthikos* (see ethic)]
study of morality's effect on conduct: the study of moral standards and how they affect conduct (*takes a singular verb*)
code of morality: a system of moral principles governing the appropriate conduct for a person or group (*takes a plural verb*)

Our behavior and actions as Clergy are always under the scrutiny of those within and outside the Path. Those within the Path are looking to us for a demonstration of leadership through example. Many outside the Path look to our actions to justify their discriminatory ideas of who we are.

As Pagans, we have undergone centuries of persecution based on misinformation and religious bias. In this modern age, there are groups of individuals who would tell others that we are 'Devil worshippers' and much worse. Yes, much of this impression is based on fear of the unknown... but strangely enough, our fellow humans will actually base ideology on constant media information, yes; movies and television.

As a Tradition, we are not here to set moral standards. Morality has never been subject to thought within the Pagan Path, that is a subject purely for the individual. Although the accepted definition seems to say otherwise, that moral view is set to a definite line... if it violates no laws (local, state or federal) and it can do no actual harm (we must never misinterpret opinion with harm), it is not of consequence to the tradition.

We as Clergy are how we are viewed as a belief system. The way we act, dress and talk. All these things have an impact.

Ethics are not just to be used in spell craft, but also in our day-to-day lives. Spreading rumors, lying and mistreating others are all unethical actions, and as such reflect upon not only the person committing these acts, but it becomes a reflection on us all as a belief system. Personally, I believe that those who try to make us look evil have enough tools found in misinformation and myth. Why give them fact-based weapons to use too?

If we as followers of the Old Ways were to practice as those before us, we could change the views of a great many people in this age. Diversity is accepted now, unlike the past. Our belief system as a whole is considered an accepted religion with all the rights bestowed on all the other religions. Now, if we were to only act the part; what an impact we could make?

The actions of the individual directly affect the level of respect they receive. An honest, ethical person is most often looked up to, while one who is not is usually shunned.

Karmic law states that our actions will be visited upon us; maybe not right away, but in time. The saying, 'What goes around, comes around,' is sort of an over simplification, but it gets the general idea across. Essentially, it says that if we live a proper life, we will be rewarded at some point. It may not occur on this plane of existence, but it will happen. Karmic law also says the same will happen for the opposite actions. In this way, Karma can be either a blessing or a curse; it is all up to you.

Anyone can call himself or herself a Wytch, but to truly be on the Path, you must subscribe to the core philosophies handed down through the centuries. Then, and only then, can you say you are a follower of the 'Old Ways'.

You have read and learned the meaning of the Witches' Rede, it teaches us honor and respect. One of the numbers of works that the Rede is based on is the Pagan Chivalric Code. It is also known as 'The Old Code'. No one knows who the author was, but it is known that it far precedes Doreen Valiente's work. Chivalry, until the Middle Ages, was practiced by all on the Path (men, women and children). Certain aspects were adopted and became part of the five Knightly Virtues. This code lays down in much more detail what Valiente summed up in eight words.

These were, in the past, words that all on the Path followed. Today it seems that most want nothing more than to say they are on the Path because it is 'cool'. I believe that to truly be among those who believe in who and what they are, you must subscribe to certain philosophies. Philosophies that the wise ones have laid down for us. Chivalry is a high code of honor, which is of most ancient Pagan origin, and must be lived by all who follow the Old Ways.

The Old Code

It must be kenned that thoughts and intent put forth on this Middle-Earth will wax strong in other worlds beyond, and return... bringing into creation, on this world, that which had been sent forth. Thus one should exercise discipline, for 'as ye do plant, so shall ye harvest.' It is only by preparing our minds to be as Gods that we can ultimately attain godhead. 'This above all... to thine own self be true...'

A Witch's word must have the validity of a signed and witnessed oath. Thus, give thy word sparingly, but adhere to it like iron. Refrain from speaking ill of others, for not all truths of the matter may be known. Pass not unverified words about another, for hearsay is, in a large part, a thing of false-hoods. Be thou honest with others, and have them know that honesty is likewise expected of them. The fury of the moment plays folly with the truth; to keep one's head is a virtue.

Contemplate always the consequences of thine acts upon others. Strive not to harm. Diverse covens may well have diverse news on love between members and with others. When a coven, clan or grove is visited or joined, one should discern quietly their practices, and abide thereby. Dignity, a gracious manner, and a good humor are much to be admired.

As a Witch, thou hast power, and thy powers wax strongly as wisdom increases. Therefore exercise discretion in the use thereof. Courage and honor endure forever. Their echoes remain when the mountains have crumbled to dust. Pledge friendship and fealty to those who so warrant. Strengthen others of the Brethren and they shall strengthen thee. Thou shall not reveal secrets of another Witch or another coven. Others have labored long and hard for them and cherish them as treasures. Though there may be differences between those of the Old Ways, those who are once born must see nothing, and must hear nothing. Those who follow the mysteries should be above reproach in the eyes of the world.

Wytches' Rede of Chivalry
The laws of the land should be obeyed whenever possible and within reason, for in the main they have been chosen with wisdom. Have pride in thyself, and seek perfection in body and in mind. For the Lady has said, 'How can thou honor another unless thou give honor to thyself first?' Those who seek the mysteries should consider themselves as select of the Gods, for it is they who lead the race of humans to the highest of thrones and beyond the very stars.
(*Unknown author*)

As you can see, there is a close parallel to the Old Code and the Rede. The true difference is found in the fact that the Code defines the way a person should act while living on the Path, where as the Rede simplifies much of what you do. Sadly, the Rede seems to have opened the door for many to use the name of Deity to give them the freedom to act in an unorthodox manner. To follow the Code closely, places us in a position to truly do no harm. This, in turn, makes us a more positive influence on the world we live in. If we incorporate the words of the code into our life, ethically we present a much more positive influence on those things and people around us.

An ethical attitude is not something that is common, yet most say they strive to achieve it. Greed, avarice, jealousy, none of which are ethical concepts, are driven into us constantly through societal manipulation. Television ads, magazine ads, the actions of others, these drive us to act unethically. Honor, respect and courtesy have been thrown to the wayside. Sadly, as Pagans, if we demonstrate the average values found in society, we are adding fuel to the fire of those who would see us no longer exist. Should we tune our minds to follow the values of our ancestors, we begin to show those things that truly have meaning.

Just taking the time to ask yourself, would I want to be treated in this manner? Simple, yet not. Because of outside influence, we have nearly stopped looking at things this way. But, if we choose to not follow the easier road, we begin to find that it starts to happen naturally. Ours is not an easy Path, there are centuries of problems to overcome. But still this is a choice we have to make. If we choose to not care about harm, then we are making things worse. If we choose to actually and consciously do no harm, then our road will be difficult but the end result will have a positive effect on all things around us.

Developing an ethical attitude may be extremely hard, but the outcome is well worth the pain. As a Pagan, the choice is yours... as a member of the Clergy; your actions affect the Path as a whole. Blessings and choose well.

Etiquette in Wytchcraft

Please, thank you, yes sir / ma'am… simple etiquette, yet it goes so much further.

Have you ever gone to an event only to find that some of the participants are just plain rude? Talking about how others are acting, the way they are dressed, etc.? Now, look at yourself. Have you ever done this? Now, have you ever gone to an event where everyone was dressed far differently than you? Maybe you are dressed way too casually or showing assets best left covered? Have you innocently made an offhand remark about someone else in attendance? Have you used profanity in front of others at an event? Have you told an 'off color' joke?

As representatives of your temple, shrine, tradition, etc. you should always present yourself in a positive light. This does not mean telling everyone how much you know or how wonderful you are, this is done by appropriate dress, manner and action. The first impression anyone has of you or the temple/tradition that you represent is your appearance. Yes, this does play into etiquette. If you enter an event dressed totally out of context with the occasion, it is considered an insult to all those in attendance that are properly attired. The second impression you will make will be based on how you act. If your actions draw attention, you may want to re-evaluate what you are doing. In some circumstances the old adage 'the squeaky wheel gets the grease' is a good thing. In most cases, however, it can cause those seeing your actions to look down not only at you, but that which your Clergy status represents.

If you tell a joke, remember the content of the joke MUST be acceptable in the company you are with. Profanity at any function is completely unacceptable! Many, even those on the Path, may find the use of profanity offensive. Remember always that you are a goodwill ambassador for the temple/tradition at all times. Anything you do or say that might offend will reflect equally on you and the temple/tradition, so act accordingly and choose your words with respect.

Pagans are notoriously late. The term 'Pagan Central Time' has come to be an almost accepted term and is the concept that things will start to happen when everyone has arrived, even if that means those who arrived at the advertised time have to wait for ages for latecomers. The bad news is, it is rude and should never be followed. If you are attending an event, workshop, class, whatever... show up on time. To think, 'oh, everybody else does it,' is an insult to your host. Some events and Rituals have started to actually close and bar the doors at the beginning of the scheduled event so that the energies present are not disrupted by a late entry.

Leave your negative energy at the door. If your frame of mind is not well grounded, it is best you pass on attending. It will affect the energies of others in attendance and generally do harm to the Ritual.

Keep your personal opinions (if they are not positive) to yourself. No two people are exactly alike and to make comments about someone in attendance will only serve to irritate others at the function. These actions will, once again, reflect negatively on the temple/tradition as well as yourself.

Using proper etiquette will ensure you are received in a more positive light, raise respect for the temple/tradition and make it more likely to be invited back for other functions. This makes you a valuable force for improved interfaith relations as well as creating an environment of growth for us all.

All of this information is quite important. However, none of this is to say that there is not a place and time for us to 'let our hair down' and have some fun. Being Pagan Clergy does not mean you have to be perfect, just aware of both circumstance and timing.

Finally, and most importantly, we will cover Circle etiquette.

As members of the Clergy, it is vital that you understand what Circle etiquette is and follow it strictly. This area is where your actions will define both you and the temple/tradition to other temples, traditions, covens, etc. Some indiscretions are easily tolerated, others are considered absolutely unacceptable for any reason, and this is one of those areas.

When attending an event and you are looking at your host's Altar, *never* under any circumstances touch any item found on the Altar without the express permission of the individual those tools belong to. As you have already learned, great time and energy is spent purifying and aligning those tools and simply picking them up without permission can render them useless until the entire blessing process has been redone. This action can ruin the Ritual and is one of the deepest insults you can give your host. The result could be your banishment from the event as well as future events by your host (word travels fast and others could join in this action).

As the Ritual begins, keep in mind, if you are not an active participant please, refrain from speaking. Ritual is an act of reverence to Deity and as such, only those who are to speak, should. When someone is speaking out of turn, it is a great distraction and can lower the energies present. This will diminish the effect and intent of the Ritual. Have the respect to simply and quietly participate. When and if there is a time for the attendees to interact, then and only then do so.

Never leave the Circle once it has been cast, unless there is an emergency! If that is the case, do not just leave, get the attention of an active participant and have them 'cut you out', this will allow the integrity of the Circle to remain intact. To do otherwise will damage the Circle and allow negative energy to enter, thereby collapsing the Circle, rendering the Ritual null.

Ethics and etiquette, as you can see, always go hand in hand. As members of the Clergy, we have the responsibility to hold the standards of our Tradition high and always act in an ethical manner and demonstrate proper etiquette at all times, not just during events, etc. We are representatives of our order 24 hours a day, not just occasionally and as such; we are subject to the appraisal of others in our day-to-day lives.

Beginning Magick

Man learns through experience, and the spiritual path is full of different kinds of experiences. He will encounter many difficulties and obstacles, and they are the very experiences he needs to encourage and complete the cleansing process.
Sai Baba

Ah, finally, Magick... Don't get your hopes up quite yet. There is much you have to learn before actually using Magick. Ethics, intent, preparation, cause and effect, so many things that are important before you do any spell work. It is important for you, as a member of Clergy, to realize that Magick is not an integral part of our Path. It is a tool, much like every other tool you have been taught about, a tool that used improperly can cause great damage.

You see that we have spelled it Magick instead of magic. There is a purpose beyond the fact that this was the early way of spelling the word. Ask yourself, 'What is Magick?' There are actually a few types of Magick.

Magic... conjuring tricks: The illusions that make apparently impossible things seem to happen, usually performed as entertainment. Essentially, these are mere parlor tricks. They use no energies or structure other than simple slight of hand. Basically, this is simple distraction and manipulation of material.

Magick... inexplicable things: A mysterious or unexplainable quality, talent or skill. The ability to use unseen energies or forces to make material change such as healing, movement, divination, etc.

Essentially Magick, as used by one on the Path, is the balancing of those energies found within yourself, coupled with the energies present around you; focused with intent to effect change. This change does not necessarily have to manifest itself in the physical. The act of casting the Circle or a sacred space is causing change in the environment found within the Circle, yet it has no visible, physical manifestation. We simply know it is there because it is felt mingling with our own internal energy. In some instances, it is quite manifest for example healing. Although this form of Magick works on a much deeper plane than the physical, it is quite readily apparent in its visible and physical results. Have you ever focused on something in your mind only to have it actually happen? In a small sense, you used energy to elicit a reaction through intent… this is Magick in its basic form.

We use some degree of Magick in the various things we do on the Path. Such as, charging and blessing the tools we use, calling the Guardians, casting the Circle. There are so many things of a Magickal nature.

The various spells available or that you can create are seemingly endless and that is why it is so important that you understand what is involved in the use of Magick.

Once more, we delve into the realm of ethics. The ethical use of Magick should be paramount to the practitioner. It goes hand in hand with the Rede and the Old Code. To cast, for example, a love spell is to bend another's will and that is a violation of the Rede. While using a spell to help you (or another) find the love that is right for you/them is not unethical. It merely aids in finding what was to be all along.

Found in today's practice of Wicca you frequently hear the phrase 'personal gain' and how bad it is. Thank you *Charmed*. That is purely a modern concept and is not wholly correct. An excerpt from an old Magickal text reads:

The Power shall not be used to bring harm, to injure or control others. But if the need arises, the Power shall be used to protect your life or the lives of others. The Power is used only as need dictates. The Power can be used for your own gain, as long as by doing so you harm none. It is unwise to accept money for use of the Power, for it quickly controls its taker. Be not as those of other religions. Use not the Power for prideful gain, for such cheapens the mysteries of the Path and Magick. Ever remember that the Power is the sacred gift of the Goddess and God, and should never be misused or abused.

And this is the Law of the Power.

The only things the Law of Power considers affronts to Deity is selling Magick, doing harm, controlling others and gain purely for pride's sake. While this does close the door to gain of wealth beyond reason and the use of Magick to line your pockets, it does not lend itself to avoiding its use to aid in your day-to-day life. Gain for survival and moderate comfort seem to be acceptable, therefore ethical. The term 'Pagan Poor' seems to be somewhat inappropriate when set to this standard.

The Law of Power also demonstrates that it is acceptable to use this power for protection from attack, be that attack on you or others. It can be used for self-defense. But it is never to be used as a tool of revenge or initial attack. It also makes it clear that use of the power to control another's will is unacceptable.

The essential fact to remember is, as in your life, you must weigh the act and determine whether that act is beneficial or can it in some way do damage. As you are beginning to learn, those truly on the Path live by a strict ethical code. As you progress along the road to Clergy status, you will see and understand why this area is so important.

The first factor in preparation of the use of Magick has already been shown to you, it must be of an ethical nature. You have determined that it is, so now we proceed. In your mind, you must develop intent. That is, visualize what it is you want to occur and see it happen. To do this, you must be aligned with your Higher

Self. Then and only then can there be any possibility of your visualization becoming manifest.

This process must be seamless in your mind and you must be able to see the outcome. If you cannot make it happen in your mind, you cannot possibly make it happen on this plane. The physical is in appearance concrete, but is actually energy. This energy is malleable but only once your Higher Self is capable of manipulating those surrounding energies. The act of energy use is in fact quite draining on the individual at first. This becomes less and less of an issue as the practitioner learns to better focus more tightly. As you learn how to do this, you actually use less energy in a more effective manner, allowing you to control both inner and outer energies with less effort and greater control.

In the beginning, even the act of casting a Circle might possibly cause a sensation of dizziness and mild euphoria. If you have attended any Rituals, I am sure you have seen how just the surrounding energies present have and can affect those just in attendance. On the novice, these energies can be quite overwhelming at times. It is for this reason that you, as that novice, work consistently with the lessons on grounding and centering, entering your Higher Self and energy raising. Doing this regularly will aid you in becoming proficient and will reduce the likelihood of fatigue.

Learn all the lessons in this book well, they will serve you well as you continue your road into the next level.

Blessings to you on your journey.

Namaste.

MOON

BOOKS

Moon Books invites you to begin or deepen your encounter with Paganism, in all its rich, creative, flourishing forms.